The Vice Chairman's Doctrine

The Vice Chairman's Doctrine

Rocking the Top in Industry Version 4.0

Ian Domowitz

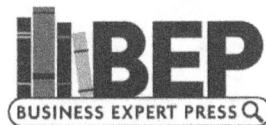

BEP
BUSINESS EXPERT PRESS
Leader in applied, concise business books

For Marguerite, whose wisdom as a CEO and life partner permeates this book. I will miss her always.

Description

There are books about product *and* companies, but no books about a company *as* a product.

After 19 years in academics and 17 years on Wall Street, Ian Domowitz arrives from orbit around the top of a corporation with a mindset of leadership without authority. The former public company Vice Chairman and CEO offers a no holds-barred treatment of influence and leverage, complete with coaching, mantras, and essential tales of leadership. Change management is a lifestyle. Transformation is a calling card. The Vice Chairman's product is the company itself.

Wrapped inside a series of vignettes, research and stories show how business process and culture converge as competitive advantage. Company priorities of innovation, branding, and culture are refashioned through unorthodox lenses that focus action through design thinking and transformation within a social system. Drawing from his body of knowledge and experience, Domowitz blurs lines between self-reflection, philosophy, and management science as he explores corporate life and decision making.

The Vice Chair learns from architects, storytellers, linguists, psychologists, relationship gurus, mathematicians, religious figures, science fiction characters, detectives, film directors, professors, entrepreneurs, software designers, fearful events, AI, and even real companies. Each teaches transformation in its own way. The greater metamorphosis combines personal development with the management of a company as though it were a product. Culture emerges in the form of actionable values.

The Vice Chairman's Doctrine is a transformative tale of leadership without authority, a perspective suiting a new breed of entrepreneurs and corporate warriors who reject control, live in a world of influencers and aspire to become one. It is a set of principles advocated, taught, and put into effect with respect to the acquisition and exercise of power, a coherent sum of assertions regarding influence and leverage within a company.

Keywords

leadership; business culture; organizational learning; management skills; design thinking; decision making; entrepreneurship; sociology; artificial intelligence

Contents

Testimonials

"*What a unique and inspired new direction for non-fiction, business-driven books.*

A masterful, thought-provoking, and engaging nonfiction read, author Ian Domowitz's The Vice Chairman's Doctrine *is a must-read business book. A brilliant deep-dive into business growth and the balance of leadership and power, the author's unique writing style, hopping back and forth between the voice of The Vice Chairman and the author himself, added humor and wit into the business-led book, creating a tone that could benefit readers of all backgrounds.*

The balance of research and development mixed with the author's unique wit and charm is what really sold this narrative."—**Anthony Alvina's Book Review Blog**

"*The Vice Chairman's Doctrine: A Guide to Rocking the Top in Industry 4.0 comes from a former public company Vice Chairman and CEO who offers a different business take than in most books. His focus on transformative business experiences, the wellsprings of creativity and flexibility that lead to success, and the stories that back these experiences set this business book apart from almost every other discussion on the market.*

Domowitz does not use a single company for his corporate examples. Instead, he weaves the perspectives, knowledge, and power of leadership and change into each different story to provide not just business lessons, but emotional connections to events and growth experiences. The addition of dramatic flourishes to capture audience attention may be otherworldly or emotional draws. But, with the best acuity of nonfiction, Domowitz supports them with real-world incidents, examples, and facts to educate and transform business readers.

It's an invitation to embrace a new form of corporate identity and excels in reframing the business perspective through a clear doctrine that defines approaches to this process. Business leaders interested in innovative concepts and creative envisioning of traditional approaches to goal attainment, adaptation, and change will welcome the stories and examples packed in an inspirational survey of many new possibilities and visions of success."—**Diane Donovan, Senior Reviewer, Midwest Book Review**

"The Vice Chairman's Doctrine is not a typical leadership or business manual. Domowitz is an articulate wordsmith who enjoys constructing a good, intellectually sound joke at his, or his industry's, expense, for an entertaining read throughout. He's able to weave different elements together, forming a comprehensive guidebook that is both immensely readable and informative. Most vitally, Domowitz possesses a charming gift for allegory, irony, and even, at times, outright satire that enhances his subject matter, making his book an entertaining and illuminating read for readers from any professional discipline."—**Self-Publishing Review**

"A masterpiece. Ian Domowitz has written a timeless manual for anyone leading and advising leaders on successful business growth and change. If wickedly erudite humor, crystal clear thinking and well-earned wisdom sound like the elements of a book you want to read, then buy The Vice-Chairman's Doctrine immediately. This is a rare, crisp exhortation I will refer to for the rest of my life."—**Jared Carney, Founder, CEO, Lightdale, LLC and Vice-Chairman, McKinley Capital**

"A must read. In ever his ever-timely book, Dr. Domowitz shares his opinion freely through his hard-earned, often gut-wrenching, insider's experience. He lays bare, from the top down, the naked, essential, often brutal elements of corporate function. Seldom can one gain an inside view of corporate intrigue and world-class wisdom at the same time. This is a no holds-barred, exceptional read, complete with coaching, mantras, and essential tales of leadership."—**Richard E. Buckley. MD, CEO, Aurora Scientific, Inc.**

"Prepare yourself for a unique journey into a forest where few dare to explore. Drawing from his body of knowledge, readings, and experience, Domowitz has blurred the line between self-reflection, philosophy, and management science and made insightful excursions into the trees and branches of corporate life and decision making. His trail guide of navigating the Industry Version 4.0 jungle and potentially finding the fruits of innovation and transformation is very fun and easy to read."—**Minder Cheng, Managing Member ThirdStream Partners and Former Chairman, Investment Technology Group, Inc.**

"Wrapped inside a series of vignettes, some humorous, some sublime, is business wisdom from someone who has 'been there and done that.' For those with the desire to lead rather than follow, this book is full of pearls that can be applied to any career at any stage."—**Richard Lindsey, Chief Investment Officer and Managing Partner, Windham Capital Management, Former President, Bear Stearns Clearing**

"Professor Domowitz has pulled off a rare feat. He's written a book that not only offers deep insights into product management and corporate culture but is genuinely a great read. Highly recommended to anyone interested in how new products and services are brought to market."—**Ananth Madhavan, Head of ETF and Index Investing Research at Blackrock and Author of *Exchange-Traded Funds and the New Dynamics of Investing***

"The Vice Chairman's Doctrine is a superb, well-written, and humorous look at the use and benefit of influence and leverage inside a corporate board room. This book is a must-read for anyone involved in corporate governance, serving on a board or leading people with or without official titles. It is also a critical learning lesson for any Chairman who has a Vice Chairman and throws away their potential for the leadership. Dr. Domowitz takes the mundane subject of corporate governance and makes it relevant and fun!"—**Robert A. Gillam, CEO and Chairman, McKinley Management, LLC**

Preface

Vice Chairman. Wow. I had to look it up.

I found distressingly little. The catch included a blurb in a 2005 issue of *Slate*, seven lines in *Wikipedia* devoted to the difference between a vice chair and executive vice president, and listings for several people with the title. I lacked even a dictionary definition of the position as described to me; a vice chair is not a deputy chairman subordinated only to the head of the board of directors.

I called a friendly executive coach, and asked her whether she, or any of her friends, had experience advising vice chairs. All they had were questions. I went back to *Slate* and the search engine.

Vice Chairman is a prestigious title, particularly in the banking and brokerage sectors. I am starting to like this.

Appointment as a Vice Chairman is typically considered to be a demotion. I am liking it less. The appointment signals a stalled career, albeit at a high level, for some indefinite period.

The Vice Chair is often an excellent golfer. This observation is as bad as the demotion. The implication is the position doesn't carry very much responsibility, and even less accountability. Office presence may be limited, and one can substitute any avocation for golf in practice.

A Vice Chairmanship may be the best job in the world. The evidence is high compensation coupled with lack of direct accountability. One cannot simply buff a resume and apply for the job. Headhunters do not recruit for this position.

The job of Vice Chairman typically goes to a top executive who has been shafted. One sympathizes. All ways in which a senior person can suffer in this fashion lead back to a single origin: reorganization. One may lose a bid to become CEO, and existing senior staff may not fit neatly into the organizational vision of the new boss. Mergers create the position, because there can only be one CEO. The loser usually heads for the proverbial hills, wherever and whatever they may be.

Vice Chairs do not write books. Yet, here we are. The presumption is no one cares what they have to say. Beyond the optics of keeping someone around, there are good reasons for the position to exist. Any Vice Chair comes equipped with a body of knowledge and experience and is a veteran of corporate committees and board rooms. Few have not commanded a small army in their history. They carry a strong personal brand and their bag of tricks includes valuable lessons for anyone at any career stage who desires to lead rather than follow.

A good Vice Chairman is that kind of magician.

Read this book, and let's have a little fun. There will be stories, even stories about stories. This is not a book about a single firm nor is it a sequence of personal war tales. You will not find four-box diagrams or bullet points in bold type. You will find the biggest mashup of transformative stories since the popular TV series Stranger Things.

Stranger Things is a tale of transfiguration. Characters and themes range from young friends struggling with identity to black-suited government agents roaming a not-so-secret secret government laboratory in which analogs of the X-Men are produced. A single mother endures the tragedy of child loss but finds help and a relationship in the form of a police chief who investigates a fearful mystery while a mad scientist creates a monster. A female lab product makes friends with all the friends, kills the monster, and strands herself in an alternative world in preparation for Season 2. A slug-like creature replaces the monster, and the audience waits with bated breath. Whew.

The series' commercial success relies on ingredients stirred together to great effect. Every characterization has an element of transformation, a universal attractor in storytelling. The assembly of transformative tales into an uneasily cohesive whole is presented as a single transformation greater than the sum of its parts. Every theme has been plumbed many times before, but each storyline has its own audience, bringing backstories and emotional response to the mix. Those in the entertainment business are rabid fans of this aspect, because a built-in audience is an easy source of revenue. Finally, the moral of the tale unfolds as another mix of ill-defined ingredients. There is no ending; a sequel awaits. Rinse and repeat.

The Vice Chairman's Doctrine is a tale of leadership without authority in which the main themes are influence and leverage. The combination of those two words generates over 100 million references in an Internet search, reflecting a lack of common definition. A mixture of design thinking and social action theory adds to the need for a dictionary, but each element has a history of extensive research, writings, and methodology. Similarly, it's hard to keep up with all the books and blogs on the topics of innovation, culture, and branding occupying the Vice Chair's attention.

We encounter architects, storytellers, linguists, psychologists, relationship gurus, mathematicians, religious figures, science fiction characters, detectives, film directors, professors, entrepreneurs, software designers, fearful events, artificial intelligence, and even real companies. Each teaches transformation in its own way. The greater transformation combines personal development with the management of a company as though it were a product. After all the work, it may still be as undefined as the current state of Industry Version 4.0. That's what sequels are for.

Any drama needs actors. The two speaking parts here are the Vice Chairman and the author. Writing in two voices is not a sign of split personality disorder, rather a way of making a point. The Vice Chair gives advice and I offer opinions. Opinions are free but frequently entertaining. Advice is educational. It also is expensive, and as such, fully deserving of your attention.

I've heard a combination of entertainment and education is a sure win.

Oh, and did I mention that the tale is about transformation? People and companies need it as we all engage with Industry 4.0.

Acknowledgments

My thanks to Ana Aisthesthai for cover art and technical support and to Jim Spohrer, former Director of Cognitive OpenTech for IBM, who reviewed the manuscript. Ananth Madhavan of Blackrock and Jack Glen of the World Bank provided helpful comments along the way. And a thank you to Scott Isenberg and the team at Business Expert Press; without them, this book would not be possible.

CHAPTER 1

The Vice Chairman
Creates a Doctrine

A Vice Chair arrives from an orbit around the top of a corporation. Backgrounds vary, but it doesn't matter. The role demands a certain mindset.

The philosophy is leadership without authority, and the ethos is product management. A product manager is the steward of a product from design through operations and sales. Product managers rarely have direct control, and no one must do what they say. Change management is a lifestyle. Transformation is a calling card.

The Vice Chair is guided by doctrine. A doctrine is a codification of beliefs or a body of instruction defined as the basis for institutional teaching with respect to internal operations. The term suggests religious or legal principles established through a history of past decisions and applies to procedures governing complex operations in warfare. All these notions can be found in the Vice Chair's philosophy comprising a set of principles advocated, taught, and put into effect with respect to the acquisition and exercise of power. It is a coherent sum of assertions regarding influence and leverage within an enterprise.

The Vice Chairman's product is the company itself. Common priorities of innovation, branding, and culture are refashioned through unorthodox lenses. The glass is ground through process, and three factories occupy the Vice Chair's attention. They are design thinking, the AGIL system of societal action, and the psychology of cognitive appraisal.

Restore a Picture by Reframing

A company consists of patterns of social behavior, and the firm functions as a society operating in the larger setting of a market. Much has been learned about societies over time, and a theory of social action is a fitting, albeit unexplored framework for corporate activity. AGIL is a systematic approach based on a hierarchy of Adaptation, Goal Attainment, Integration, and Latency.[1] Culture is the embodiment of latent patterns within a firm and exercises cybernetic control over components of the system while flowing from values through rituals all the way to symbols associated with branding.

Adaptation is the capacity to interact with the environment for the purpose of resource management and production, while Goal Attainment motivates and guides the organization. Integration regulates the activities of diverse stakeholders and demands convergence of values and norms with those of the company. Latency is shorthand for latent pattern maintenance defined as the preservation of behavioral patterns necessary for company survival. These patterns are products of action and conditioning influences for future activity.

A complementary perspective casts a company as a set of problems looking for a set of solutions. Innovation is a problem-solving exercise resulting in product, service, or structure that creates value, for example. We interrogate problems to determine a frame and a logical progression for critical thought, and creative thinking is the discovery of a concept that links a set of problems to a set of solutions. The framework for this exercise is design reasoning.

Design thinking is having its day in business analytics, and published variants offer several prescriptive phases very similar across treatments. A fan of simplicity, the Vice Chair has only a single line to read: *What + How = Value*. The focus is on problems for which only value is well defined, a commonplace circumstance in innovation efforts. Establishment of a frame for experimentation leading to solutions of ill-defined problems provides the lens through which problems are solved.

Design thinking is a cultural guide in which process and culture come together as competitive advantage.

The concept is customer-centric and requires a certain amount of empathy. Empathy derives not only from common experience, but also from recognition and appreciation of emotions. Emotional ability in business is hailed as EQ. We rarely define this prized personal asset but claim to recognize the quality when we see it. In practice, we require a frame for thinking about emotion generated through action tendencies. They are easier to observe and comprehend.

We decide how an event makes us feel through interpretation. We assess relevance along dimensions of motivation, value, accountability, and responsibility. Accountability is a logical exercise, but responsibility entails an emotional commitment.

A Social Engineer Manipulates Myth

Emotion brings us to branding. Brand recognition is about why the company exists, and any question of *why* is seated in the emotional aisle of the brain. Branding is a social engineering exercise constituting a direct appeal to emotion through customers' appraisal, leading to the action tendency of loyalty.

Brands are distinguished from advertising schemes as credible by embodying the cumulative effect of marketing over time. Brand consumers provoke new interpretation of those activities with every new generation. Brand positioning may change, but new interpretations cannot threaten the consistency of the brand, creating the sort of paradox addressed in design thinking. A frame for its resolution is one of transformation.

Transformation is more than a story about singular circumstances and involves the myth that transformation itself can be managed on behalf of the customer. This myth may serve as the brand itself. Why does the company exist? The answer better be about transformation.

Myth is a form of narrative, and narrative is a discipline.

The goal of stories is the sale of ideas. Good stories have questions to answer. Good answers support broad story lines, and general narrative provides a deeper foundation for influence. Conventional executive rhetoric is too logical to be inspiring: stories resonate with the emotional part of our being, and culture is driven by emotion not logic. The idea and the emotion in any tale should be united.

The language of stories brings new definitions. Definitions change the topology of influence, and the emotional trappings of language are channels through which we change culture. Word invention can be elevated beyond obscure jargon to the art of explaining entire strategies through a single term. The process explains or justifies personal and corporate brand positioning if done correctly.

Language morphs into cultural bullet points advocated by management and sold by human resource departments, but the Vice Chair is interested in the fundamentals of cultural change as opposed to motivating slogans. If you want to know about culture, listen to the stories. If you want to change culture, change the process. Better stories will follow.

Teachers of Process as Culture

Process as culture is exemplified in behavioral traits of other species. Three find a place in the Vice Chair's thinking.

Successful married couples constitute a unique species operating outside the workplace. Marriage is a process of evolving cultural accommodation, a mechanism poorly understood in corporate merger activity. Marriage and corporation depend on social contracts, and examples of successful contracts manifest in the way couples interact.

Couples trade and negotiate tradeoffs. Trading translates value into prices and assigns those prices to intermediate steps toward a long-run goal. Successful tradeoffs depend on economic principles underlying the subjective notion of caring within human relationships. Our world is no longer solely occupied by humans, however.

Bumper stickers proclaim, HIRE THE ARTIFICIALLY INTELLIGENT.

Such creatures are not uncommon. They represent characters possessed of problem-solving architecture, leading us into the Fourth Industrial Revolution—Industry Version 4.0.

The Machine Age brought about a restructuring of society through mechanics and electricity. Artificial intelligence forces a culture shift because it alters the relationship between data and humans, changing machines from passive to active players. The artificially intelligent teach culture through process and innovation through design.

Struggles of innovation within corporate structures are examined through the study of the rarest species of all, the *intrapreneur*.

Intrapreneurship represents entrepreneurial innovation within established companies. It is treated as venture creation, and the setting provides a basis for looking at innovation not as product or service, rather as a process coherent within an enterprise structure.

The intrapreneur sees transformation. The potential may always have existed or it may be of the moment. The intrapreneur tells a story of transformation, which is credible and thus sets about the task cultivating influence to create leverage necessary for implementation.

Combining Influence and Leverage Delivers Interesting Results

Value creation without direct authority teaches the importance of credibility, influence, and leverage. It also teaches lessons about power.

Legitimate power is useful only if influencers do their work by making others believe in a title and position. Informational power becomes credible as intelligence successfully passes on to others inside and outside the company. Referent power inspires a larger population by leveraging a combination of myth and purpose.

Influence and leverage find expression in the cybernetic system of functions within a company. In any cybernetic scheme, a function is in control of the one beneath it. Control is expressed through the concept of *definition*. Senior management follows a sequence: cultural pattern maintenance defines integration; integration defines goals; and goals drive adaptation. Definition is an explanation of the nature or essential qualities of a thing; "to define functions" is the dictionary example. Definition also includes fixing the boundaries of a function.

A leader defines but does not determine. Determination is to cause, affect, or decide causally. The legitimate power granted to the leader may fool one into thinking determination is therefore on the leader. Good companies, like good societies, do not function in such a fashion.

One function defines another in the same way as computer code defines a game. The program does not determine the game. Actual outcomes depend on the players. Determination is to come to a resolution and is a conclusion reached after reasoning and observation. This is not the role of the leader; rather what employees do. The leader defines the game and influences others to determine a mutually satisfactory conclusion based on the rules.

We shape worker imagination to achieve a collective determination. We follow the cybernetic hierarchy inherent in the company cum society in order to be effective. We leverage not only employees and their human capital commitment, but also the processes inherent in the definition of company functions.

We define culture and leverage it through process.

The Vice Chairman lives to play the game, and The Great Game is the life we all choose as agents of business. The contest is not about control. Coercive power is a loser and largely irrelevant in day-to-day trials. Leverage is discipline in the form of deployment of multiple hands and minds for the achievement of goals suggested in the game of ideas. Credibility and influence are in the vanguard.

Influence and leverage constitute a lifestyle. Welcome to the Vice Chairman's life.

CHAPTER 2

The Gray Man

The new CEO had been in the chair for almost a year. I was in the seat facing him for our first weekly meeting in January. Company compensation had been decided, and budgets, with the inevitable encyclopedia of spreadsheets, were in. Prepared for a grilling on the year's prospects for my subsidiary, I was relaxed and ready to go. It was not to be.

The beginning of the conversation came across as, garble garble garble…reorganization, garble garble…and you become Vice Chairman of the company. The Vice Chair parses long paragraphs in favor of the important bits. I decided on a Socratic approach.

Does the position entail a board seat? No.

Did you speak with the Chairman about this? Yes, but I don't need permission.

How might we deal with the employees? The clients will understand what it means more than the people within the company.

Hmmm.

The Vice Chairman adapts quickly to circumstances. The trick is to be always in the mood, whatever mood suits the occasion and whatever the occasion. Time to switch gears.

What about staffing? This is a standalone position, but I don't expect you to do your own spreadsheets or to code for research purposes. Your team loves you, and you can certainly get a cycle or two out of people.

I offered a two-sentence refresher on prioritization within an ongoing strategic operating plan. Following acknowledgment of difficulties, I immediately requested an individual of my choice, and not a junior staffer, either.

The response? I'm impressed you put it on the table so quickly.

Timing is everything, as the saying goes. Time to end this conversation with a grace period "to think about it" and come back to discuss expectations more fully. Too many corporate meetings end this way, but on this occasion, I appreciated the formality.

Shades of Gray

The Vice Chairman plans slowly and acts quickly.

Any rule is characterized by its exceptions. The first decision of the newly anointed was to ignore this advice. The CEO had preached a sense of urgency for the past year, but what was truly desired was immediacy. There was work to do.

Years had been spent building a talented and discreet management team. I called them together and broke the news. Within a day, the group tied up financials with a bow, annotated and ready to hand over. I consulted the team with respect to candidates for promotion, identified potential country relocation for senior folks, and drafted a fresh global organizational structure for consideration.

The Vice Chairman favors the military dictum: never leave a person behind.

On the third day, I held a global town hall for those in the subsidiary and others maintaining close working relationships with them. Two people new to the firm divided up my old job and were invited. This is not retirement, I said, almost choking on it. I asked the incoming managers to say a few words. They spoke little. In fairness, they had only been recently informed themselves. The contrast with my own unprepared speech lifted my spirits but only slightly.

The fourth morning found me back in the CEO's office. I reported. He was mildly surprised. Formalities remaining consisted of signing over my existing CEO/President positions and board directorships within the larger corporation. The legal machine would grind this out in advance of the next proxy statement.

I became the Gray Man.

I attended meetings, but few invitations appeared in my inbox. Email traffic slowed perceptibly. I came and went almost without notice. There was real work to do were I to avoid disappearing into the proverbial woodwork.

Have you ever entertained the question, if I began a corporate career and knew what I know today, what would I do?

At a young age, facing a new job that is not well understood, with no subordinates and uncertain expectations ... scary. Thin out the hair and we have the freshly minted Vice Chairman. The description also sounds like an entrepreneur with experience, a fresh slate, and funding. I'm feeling better already. Experience dictates the first task, the setting of priorities.

Desires Dictate Priorities, Priorities Shape Choice, and Choice Defines Action

The Vice Chairman believes in the gospel of three priorities and 100 clients. Three themes are fewer than recommended by some, but a small number is useful discipline. The editing exercise permits narrow goals to fit a broader vision. A limitation to major clients is pragmatism in terms of time management and financial reward.

Priorities must suit context. We were two quarters into a ten-quarter strategic plan, and many companies fail at effectively integrating tactical solutions with an infrastructure rebuild. The strategic plan is a machine mowing down everything in its path despite the obvious: one is fixing a moving ship. This is hardly a new observation.

Star Trek's Chief Engineer Scotty did have a new thought as he discovered trans warp drive, exclaiming, it never occurred to me that space is moving, not the star ship. This single comment born of hours of reruns conquered boredom. The implications led to goal setting within a stationary company in markets moving through and around it.

The first priority is content and product, albeit not the most important of the three. It comes first, because the Gray Man can immediately add value along those dimensions while remaining, well, gray. Content in the form of research and the selling of ideas is new by definition. Content is good if it leads to new product.

Some call this innovation, and it can be accomplished on an otherwise stationary ship.

Innovation is a problem-solving exercise transforming product, brand, service, or business model in such a way as to create value. Incremental innovation is the art of using existing technology to increase value within an established market. The Gray Man cannot spend time on existing product, however. The strategic plan has contingencies for each one, and those decisions have been made by others. One cannot be both gray and operational at the same time.

Disruptive innovation involves applying new technology or novel business model to the company's current market. Value is known, because you are in the same market as before within the same competitive environment. The choice is what technology or business model to apply, and sometimes both are relevant.

Architectural innovation is adoption of known principles and technology and their application to a different market, although some use the term in reference to component infrastructure. The value proposition often is missing in that case. There is no time for missing value propositions. Ignorance of value is too big a business risk to consider.

The Vice Chair is concerned with radical innovation.

Value is perceived, but product and operating principle are lacking. Radical innovation is not just about vision and its implementation. It is generated by logical contradictions in workplace practice and paradoxes in product and market. Resolution of paradox through frames designed for experimentation defines the solution set to business problems.

Industry Version 4.0 is characterized by technologies that obscure boundaries between the physical, digital, and biological, and artificial intelligence (AI) births much of the radical innovation these days. Like any newly delivered baby, AI lives in a world of trial and error. Framing problems becomes a competitive imperative in which creativity is a process for which trial and error constitute experimentation. Willingness to experiment is not part of all corporate value systems, but AI will get us there.

Branding is the second priority. Marketing is for the masses; selling is directed at a select few; but the brand instills the purpose of a company into both. The brand evolves slowly as the market passes through the company and constitutes a manifestation of social engineering to achieve a credible presence that attracts and retains customers.

Customers don't buy a product or service. They buy a result.

The *why* behind generation of the result is the brand. If the product is a company, the brand is why the company exists. The *why* is the basis of the Vice Chairman's low-tech branding approach to high-tech Industry 4.0. Retaining identity remains the key issue in a world in which digital technology encourages rapid creativity and promotes the concept of fluid branding.

Programmatic brand management is possible, and personalized brand characters driven by machine learning are the rage as companies attempt to address different audience segments simultaneously. Are you a broker, a technology firm, a network provider, a content producer, consultant, or aggregator? All the above in some companies. Roles based upon what the company provides may be misleading, and the *why* must apply to all segments to be memorable.

The third priority is culture, the generator of more literature than the Vice Chair wants to read. Culture consists of patterns of social behavior. Company practice is grounded in values, imprinted through rituals, and communicated through symbols. Cultural systems may be considered as products of action or as conditioning influences for future action.

Culture is a manifestation of cybernetic control in which values and norms surrounding venture, product, or innovation are made convergent with those of the company. Goal attainment is defined based on those norms. Adaptation is a process of creating product based on goals and the values established at various stages of cultural development.

Louis Gerstner famously said, the thing I have learned at IBM is that culture is everything. Companies may share this mindset in the form of goal setting to include breaking down silos, collaboration across regions and functions, and conquering a lack of engagement with peers around the company. These are the results of cultural change, however. They are not guiding principles.

Gerstner's principle is to integrate as a team within the company so the company can integrate for customers on their own premises. Rather than fixate on strategy, the firm views process and culture as strategic competitive advantage. Definition and determination of culture come together through process, which in turn yields advantage.

Process as culture is a result.

Social engineering is the frame adopted for the design of culture. Preaching culture is often done logically, but delivering cultural change is channeled through an appeal to emotions. Social engineering is rarely a logical exercise, and design reasoning begins with the same premise, exhibiting a shift from product and service to a set of customer problems and solutions. The process requires empathy. Definitions morph into stories, stories to concept, design to experiments and ultimately scale in production. Do this consistently, and a culture of creativity and teamwork emerges. The contribution is actionable cultural icons of problem-solving, continuous learning, experimentation, value creation, innovation, change management, persistence, and efficiency.

The Vice Chairman is certain a company's primary goals will remain innovation, culture, and branding in Industry Version 4.0.

The Vice Chair as Product Manager

The priorities fit into a bigger picture and are in tune with current context and expected circumstance. Why the company exists is integrated into the branding exercise. How we get there is driven by a shift to design thinking and cultural change through social engineering. Innovation in the form of actionable tactics constitutes value creation.

It takes a certain mindset to handle the job, and a useful guide is product management. Few Vice Chairs grow up as product managers, but it is the general description and characteristics that matter. Product managers are known for the problems they choose to solve, not just by providing a quality fix to problems created by others.

A product manager is shepherd of a product from idea inception through development to marketing and sales and finally to enhancement and maintenance. The product manager often has no direct reports, and the philosophy is leverage rather than control. Credibility and influence are in the vanguard.

A product manager leads without authority, and the concept of leadership absent control is familiar in other contexts. Prophets lead but have no ability to compel followers to comply with their teachings. Disciples nevertheless do so. Prophecies are transformative by design and therein lies part of the prophet's influence. A business consultant also fits the description. Accenture, for example, leads companies through phases of development and crises, but a firm does not have to do what they say. Transformation is in the form of novel company processes and a new image.

Designers produce systems. Software engineers produce computer code. The outputs of product managers are frameworks for solving problems, how a team communicates, and the way in which decisions are made.

This is often called *process*. Process varies, but includes a scheme for problem identification, understanding of the issue, devising a plan, and carrying out the plan.

Product managers communicate across different functions. This involves enough expertise in design, engineering, and support services to know how to listen. Effective listening is followed by thoughtful questioning. Responses are generated in the form of stories.

Storytelling is an essential talent for the product manager.

Good managers are great at narrative. Narratives nest process by guiding understanding as to why particular product decisions are taken and what consequences are likely. They articulate how customers perceive value, why engineers and designers do what they do within scope, and how the product will create value for business and customer alike.

A great manager is one who can tell stories about the process itself. Those tales should be told early and often.

What little is written about product management emphasizes a lack of decision-making power. The ultimate authority to "make the call" is not in the job description. In a world of imperfect information, however, the product manager has learned to make decisions, being flexible and methodical in gaining experience from mistakes.

Decision making requires knowledge about when and how to use singular strategies for learning or problem-solving. Some ascribe this to a form of thinking introduced by developmental psychologist John Flavell in the mid-1970s.[1]

Metacognition entails content knowledge and an understanding of capabilities. Task knowledge follows from experience, comprising how one perceives the difficulty of a job. Strategic knowledge manifests itself through a capability for employing diverse tactics to gather information. The product manager knows how to design and analyze experiments that inform all of these elements.

We perform experiments in response to demands for change. The product manager seeks insights about customer needs and corrects course to suit. Intracompany reorganizations beyond the manager's control force similar course corrections as the product manager goes about the tasks of facilitating and coordinating the way forward.

The Vice Chairman's product is the company itself.

The product manager's integrity and interpersonal skills are key components of the personality. So, let's go crash some meetings beginning with product development. The Vice Chairman does not look good in gray.

Chapter Notes

The title comes from *The Man in the Gray Flannel Suit*. You must be of a certain age to get the joke. Like, old enough to still wear a suit.

Dallin Harris Oaks is an American jurist, educator, and religious leader, who is responsible for the original epigram of desires and priorities. His motto is "Work first, play later." His family says they are tempted to change it to: "Work first, play never." Even religious figures make mistakes.

CHAPTER 3

The Cult of Great Ideas

Jean Renoir wrote a letter to Ingrid Bergman, saying "The cult of great ideas is dangerous and may destroy the real basis for great achievements, that is the daily, humble work within the framework of a profession." As an artist, he commended humility to other artists. As a businessperson, he introduced two concepts at the heart of modern innovation within companies: great ideas are not enough; innovation is a joint effort.

The Vice Chairman likes good ideas but opposes fundamentalist beliefs. The tendency to worship ideas creates critical blindness. Blindness leads to orthodoxies leading to imprinting ideas rather than formulating experiments and tests. The sheer number of ideas rules in brainstorming sessions. Trophies are given out for participation, not for solving problems.

The research of Linda Hill is a modern twist on Renoir, focusing on leadership of innovation.[1] Her lessons are those of collective effort, as opposed to solo idea generation. A marketplace of ideas is not about brainstorming, rather amplification of differences within a portfolio of ideas. She invokes design thinking as a guide to testing and refining the portfolio. Pilots are tossed aside as being all about being correct while experiments are in.

Hill eschews the notion of a visionary in favor of the leader as an architect. An example of Pixar paints the boss as creating a studio in the form of a public town square, but inspirational examples often lack guidance. Design thinking is a case in point.

The Problem Is the Way We See the Problem

Design thinking is a paradigm for dealing with problems, not ideas. The mathematician George Pólya is arguably the first to formalize its reasoning, although he is never mentioned in modern definitions of the process. He identifies four principles of problem-solving.

Begin with understanding the problem. It seems so obvious it is often missed.

Pólya detailed questions to be addressed. The ability to physically write the problem and conditions constraining the solution is mandatory and requires more than a few notes on a white board. Do you understand all the words used in stating the problem, and can you restate the problem in your own words? What is unknown here, and does the nature of the conditions suffice to determine the unknown?

Pólya notes there are many reasonable ways to solve problems. His second principle is just as matter of fact.

Devise a plan.

Find the connection between data and the unknown. Can you derive something useful from the data? Can you think of other data appropriate to determine the unknown? You may consider auxiliary problems if an immediate connection cannot be found. A few questions eventually should lead to a plan, and Pólya suggests a few.

Try to think of a familiar problem having a similar unknown. Have you seen it before, or have you seen the same problem in a slightly different form? Do you know a related problem? Could you use its method of solution?

He included a rather radical thought, oddly appropriate 75 years after initial publication. Can you change the unknown or data, or both if necessary, to make the new unknown and new data are nearer to each other? Some problems in artificial intelligence and climate change are particularly susceptible to such an approach.

The third principle is, *carry out the plan.*

At this stage, it may be easier done than said. Add care and patience to the necessary skills. Persist until the solution, or a new plan, presents itself.

Even mathematicians seek solutions by trial and error in the form of a series of experiments. Each probe attempts to correct errors committed by the preceding. Pólya used the mathematical term *successive approximations* to capture the notion. Trials come closer and closer to the desired result. Pólya did not discourage his students from using trial and error; on the contrary, he encouraged intelligent use of the fundamental method of successive approximations. Yet he convincingly showed "for ... many ... situations, straightforward algebra is more efficient than successive approximations."[2] A single formula may trump a series of small steps.

The final principle is important in business applications.

Look back. What worked, and what did not?

Can you use the result, or the method, for some other problem? Tactical examples are building blocks for successful problem-solving strategies.

The Grand Thing Is to Be Able to Reason Backward

The modern version of Pólya's principles is called *design thinking.*

Management consultants, innovation instructors, and software developers rush in to supply definitions and toolboxes. The emphasis often is on the ideas, sometimes on the process, and occasionally on the problem. Idea management software boasts coded generation of large numbers of ideas.

Design thinking sounds like agile programming in software design. Both constitute an iterative process in which we seek to understand the user, examine assumptions, and redefine problems. Proponents profess a deep interest in understanding the people for whom products or services are crafted. The goal is observation and the development of empathy with the user. Design teaches framing problems in customer-centric ways, creating many ideas via brainstorming, and adopting an approach to prototyping and testing.

Variants of the process have from three to over a dozen phases. Begin with describing the users' needs and issues by empathizing with prospective customers. The word *ideate* appears next as a catch-all for creating ideas leading to innovative solutions. Prototyping follows and solutions are tested. Rinse and repeat. Pólya is recast with a bit of sociology and released from any mathematical constraints.

The Vice Chairman interrogates a problem to determine a frame and a logical progression for critical thought. Creative thinking is defined by the discovery of a concept that links a set of problems to a set of solutions.

Keep the key words in mind: problems, concept, solutions, logic, and questioning. I don't see the word, *idea*, here. Kees Dorst offers a corresponding foundation of applied design thinking suitable for all business applications.[3]

We solve problems by looking at the knowns and unknowns in the equation:

WHAT   +   HOW   leads to   VALUE
(thing)   (working principle)   (observed or aspirational)

If one replaces *value* by *result,* but considers the result as unknown, we have prediction. The outcome of a business practice is conceived in terms of value, however, and practitioners see no question mark here. We are here to add value, and typically understand how value is measured.

In conventional problem-solving, the value is known, as is the *how,* the working principle. What is missing is the *what,* whether a product, a service, or a system:

???   +   HOW   leads to   VALUE

Engineers create a design based on a known operating principle within a scenario of value creation. Companies engage in this practice daily. A dynamic environment may recast the value, even the how, but we plug those in and keep at it.

Sometimes we know what to produce to add value but are unsure of the principle within which to create it. Then,

WHAT   +   ???   leads to   VALUE

This formulation nests the case in which the service may already be in production, but one is looking for a more efficient cost structure. It also encompasses situations encountered when contemplating changes in the way components of a product are linked together while leaving the core design untouched. Value is described as a decrease in cost or an incremental improvement in efficiency lowering the cost of capital. A new principle is required.

Design thinking is concerned with a seemingly unsolvable problem, having one equation with two unknowns:

$$??? \quad + \quad ??? \quad \text{leads to} \quad \text{VALUE}$$

We need to figure out *what* to create. There is no established, or at least chosen, working principle that can guide the choice nor lead to expected value.

Change the Frame

Brainstorming is a process by which people randomly choose pairs for both the *how* and the *what*. The goal is a matching pair leading to the aspired value, but the process is inefficient at best. Pólya understood this when recommending straightforward algebra over successive approximations. Algebra cannot solve a single equation in two unknowns, however.

Experienced designers seek a *frame*.

The frame is a statement requiring a specific perception of a problem situation. Enunciation of a frame embodies a working hypothesis: if one looks at the problem from a certain viewpoint and adopts a working principle associated with the view, then value is created. The design problem then reverts to *what* is to be built. Only complete equations can be tested, and until the test, the frame is simply a possible way forward. At Pixar, for example, no part of a movie is considered finished until the movie wraps.

Observation leading to the emergence of themes permitting frame development is not haphazard, illustrated by a problem from the Designing Out Crime Centre in the United Kingdom.[4]

An outer metropolitan area with bars and clubs is crowded with young people each night. The district is characterized by drunkenness, theft, and occasional violence. Local authorities increasingly rely on police presence and regulations requiring massive amounts of private security. These measures do not deliver a successful outcome.

Authorities framed the issues as law-and-order problems, therefore requiring law-and-order solutions. The entertainees were predominantly noncriminals wanting to have a good time, however, and a good time was the value to be achieved. The failure to get a good experience was at odds with the nature of the area and exacerbated by the harsh security measures.

The designers reframed the problem by proposing the analogy of a music festival. What would one do if one organized such an event? The frame led to multiple design directions, of which three are illustrative.

Event organizers must guarantee people could get there and leave safely when desired. The designers noticed peak entry times were between midnight and 1:00 a.m., but the last train left at 1:20 a.m. Cabs disappeared by that time, and the youths straggled until trains started again at 6:00 a.m. Delays were a source of frustration and aggression. The designers put signage on the pavement guiding a walk to a 24-hour train, which otherwise was not obvious but constituted a simple, effective, and feasible alternative to rescheduling train service.

There would be areas to chill and continuous attractions away from a main stage in a festival. The entertainment quarter was limited to a few big clubs as the main attractions, however. Leaving one club for another was frustrated by long lines, resulting in people wandering the streets. The designers suggested an app permitting revelers to check waiting lines before leaving a venue combined with the opening of a few lanes around the clubs as rest areas with benches and tables.

Safety and guidance are key elements of any fest, but the answer did not lie in more bouncers. Adopting the festival practice of easily identifiable young guides in the area (read, bright T-shirts) leads to help when needed. Bouncers can stay; you always need them, no matter how hard you try.

You Know My Methods. Apply Them

Sherlock Holmes said his method of detection was founded upon the observation of trifles. He criticized Dr. Watson for seeing but failing to observe.

From Sherlock's perspective, product design methodology such as QFD, quality function deployment, or TIPS, the theory of inventive problem-solving, have a key shortfall. They begin with theory, blend in the problem, and deduce the outcome while following an outline of steps necessary to achieve it.

Contrary to popular belief stoked by Holmes' soliloquies, Sherlock did not practice deduction, rather *induction*.

Deduction is axiomatic, while induction depends on imperfect data. An inductive argument is affected by acquiring new evidence, but a deductive argument is not. The former is intended to be compelling; if the premises are true, it is unlikely the conclusion is false. The strength of the argument depends on the quantity and quality of input data.

Design reasoning is inductive in nature. Observation and experimentation are key components. New data may be used to validate a design thesis, or they may contribute to the discovery of themes, which aids in the identification of working principles. In practice, we need both.

Consider the observation and conclusion: every time I've walked the dog, the cat next door hasn't tried to claw me. So, the next time I walk the dog, the neighbor's cat won't scratch me.

The data consist of my experiences in dog walking. The argument is stronger the more times I walk the dog. Now comes the test. I walk the dog one day and the neighbor's pet door is closed; no scratch. The next time, the door is open, and my pants are in tatters. The principle of walking must incorporate the neighbor's schedule in order to avoid going to the haberdasher. Modify the working principle and try again. The cost of pants also suggests spending some resources in gathering more data about the cat's behavior.

A more realistic example comes from a personal experience at one of those three-letter agencies. I worked a desk devoted to Soviet surface-to-surface mobile missiles. My beat was East Germany and Czechoslovakia, populated by multiple Soviet armies at the time. The job was challenging and satisfying, but there was a problem. I liked to play guitar at local clubs, and movement of nuclear-tipped weapons was a nighttime activity. I needed a day job.

My search led me to intelligence gathering with respect to mobile surface-to-air missiles (SAMs). It was considered boring work, but I could sense the coming of the 1973 war in the Middle East, and the Soviets supplied the heavy guns. SAM batteries could only exercise when the sun was over the horizon. I had my day job.

Soviet SAM regiments protected combat zones by an air defense network. They were secretive in communications and stealthy in movement. Value was defined as actionable intelligence concerning equipment, tactics, communications protocols, and knowledge of mobile battery placements for purpose of destruction.

My predecessors defined the *how* of things in terms of signal intelligence harvested during regimental exercises. Information was gathered through an element of the Iron Horse antennae network, an array capable of locating high-frequency transmissions from anywhere on the planet. Iron Horse consisted of eight circular antennas positioned around the globe by the National Security Agency during the Cold War for search of high-priority targets through signal intelligence. My piece was the Elephant Cage, over a quarter mile in diameter and 120 feet high. Now decommissioned, the Cage was a sight to see.

The existing frame consisted of armywide exercises within which SAM activity could be detected. Regular army communication channels tipped potential availability of SAM intelligence. No one knew how to detect regimental movement and signaling outside of army movements. Armywide exercises were relatively infrequent, and intelligence was scarce. My immediate predecessor feared the lack of hard intelligence was career-limiting. He was happy to move on.

Overflights defined a new frame. SAM batteries had to target something, and the link between *how* and *value* permitted experimentation beyond army exercises. Many planes flew through Soviet airspace every day, and the first experiment collated data on commercial flight plans with high frequency direction finding. Complete and utter failure.

One does not throw away a frame because of a failed experiment. The whole point of a frame is to permit discovery of a new *what-how* combination. Never mind how or exactly why, but on my way to speak with Air Force personnel, I came across an abandoned sheaf of paper covered with garble. I was told it arrived every morning but was regarded as low-level traffic, and no one had ever bothered to decode it. It took less than a day to do so.

The garble consisted of flight plan information for Soviet transports passing through East German airspace. I watched the flights; so did the SAM batteries. Repeated episodes provided a correlation with previously unintelligible chatter. As the planes moved, deployment and targeting instructions came over in bits and pieces. Patterns emerged. In the new frame, the *how* became military flight tracking, combined with statistical analysis of movement and tactics. The *what* turned into real-time analysis of signal intelligence.

My band signed a contract with a local club.

Paradox

When does a product team adopt what first may appear to be a process of guessing games? The problem situation presents a *paradox*, an opposition of views, approaches, or requirements. Framing is a response to paradox. Sometimes we search for it. Other times, the paradox is obvious. A common example involves a successful business for which growth has slowed perceptibly. How can you be successful if you are not growing?

My team once faced several issues perceived as inhibiting growth, although the operation succeeded by typical vanity metrics. Third-party surveys said we held from 45 to 55 percent of the market in our industry segment. The subsidiary was globalized. Revenue was substantial and profit margins good. The occasional price war was a feature of the competitive environment, but we remained the premium provider and charged for it. We enjoyed a 5 percent client attrition rate annually, within norms for a subscription business. New sales made up the shortfall every year, but we had stopped growing.

The team blamed a gap in the subsidiary's commercial strategy. Individual members had different gaps in mind.

Several fingers pointed at marketing. The marketing machine served the parent company brand. Product marketing was out, while new corporate slogans, brand colors, and art at corporate headquarters were in. Content was expected by clients in the subsidiary's segment, and content marketing was considered a key component by the team. It was lacking. The larger corporation was sending out logo-branded toys, mousepads, and Rubik cubes.

Other fingers pointed to lack of a direct link between sales and marketing efforts. The Financial Engineering group produced more than enough content, but consultants did not pass it along in such a manner as to deepen client relationships and sell product. The consultants retorted by citing a lack of commercial bent in Financial Engineering, making it impossible to sell the ideas as presented back to them. Discussions went downhill from there.

Friendly debate resurfaced based on input from client service personnel and the product team. Client community-building was considered an integral part of a lock-in strategy. Everyone agreed, but it did not seem to fit with other issues in the team's collective mind.

The situation fits within the framework of design thinking. There is a paradox. A set of problems is identified. The potentially conflicting nature of the problems makes a single concept linking them to solutions nebulous at best. We don't know what to build, and we don't have an underlying principle linking the *what* to *value*.

We needed a frame.

Previous principles used to design sellable product produced revenue but not value in terms of growth. A new frame nestled in the area of team agreement: interactivity and community development across and within a broad client base. The team went so far as to suggest the interactivity should be across company personnel in addition to being enjoyed by clients, prospects, and influencers.

The usefulness of any frame lies in the isolation of a working principle—the *how*. The principle emerged as *social engineering* once engagement was adopted as a frame.

The term sounds bad based on the first 50 or so items in an Internet search. It is a psychological attack vector that relies on human interaction and involves tricking people into breaking normal security protocols.

Hackers have something to teach us. Social engineering is the modern art of mass influence abetted by a human–machine interface and using a combination of psychology and technical tools. The activity influences a person to take an action that may or may not be in their best interest. Let's assume the best.

The frame and emerging principle are not meant to generate ideas. They constitute a means to experiment with them and to test their validity. A pragmatic approach to a test bed is required.

We built a website that lived in the cloud outside the corporate firewall. It could be accessed by anyone on any mobile device or desktop. One signed in through social media sites such as Facebook.

The Analytics Incubator was born.

The first tab of the site led to interactive prototypes built by Financial Engineering. Tests of business hypotheses, early customer feedback, and determination of product market fit were possible. Small groups could move quickly and connect directly with customers. Development teams accomplished speedy iterations enabled through feedback and a lightweight software release procedure. We later learned Microsoft built the Garage, serving thousands of employees, on the same principle.

Financial Engineering was encouraged to produce prototypes as opposed to concept papers. Consultants and sales personnel used the prototypes at the customer site, permitting the client or prospect to play with the tools and ask questions at the same time. The human–machine interplay became an influencer. An indirect link between sales and marketing was established.

Social engineering is designed to make people act and must include a link to tangible items and immediate reward. A rare commodity—proprietary data—occupied the second section of the site. Financial Engineering fully explicated the data sets underlying the prototype apps. The data could be downloaded in easy-to-process form for any use.

What idea was being tested here? The data sets were limited in scope but usable for applications. Larger and more complete data sets could be obtained at a price, providing a direct link between sales and the marketing tool.

A third section contained research papers underlying the prototypes and using the data. Nothing new here: we produced such content as part of normal operations. Curated, however, the publications explained the problem at hand and illustrated the value of the data. The apps provided physical support for the research. The Incubator traced a concept through data and application all the way to presentation of actionable information.

Any content website has a community page. The hope was the common experience across the apps would generate outside interaction in the form of posts and questions. This interaction would create community.

We forgot something. Social engineering requires direct stimulus, and the community initiative failed. We needed more experiments.

The page was linked to a Twitter feed with a sexy moniker. We disseminated news in the form of unusual market conditions and the direction of global market openings every day. We advertised new research and apps on Twitter.

The Analytics Incubator community doubled almost overnight. A campaign to produce content in the form of "the question of the week" with illustrated data-driven answers was undertaken. Subscription to the site doubled again, and sales began to be made from the Incubator leads and prospect discussions. We were rolling.

Process as Culture

First comes the value aspiration, followed by a frame, then a principle. Only then can ideas be tested. In this case, there was an unexpected bonus. The process changed culture and served as an internal learning mechanism.

The larger corporation split deeply along geographical and business lines at the time of the initial Incubator build. The concept required some selling across the divides.

Once explained, a volunteer army stepped out of the shadows. Representatives from Compliance, Security, Technology and even the front office collaborated. The effort was global, and silos disappeared when Incubator was discussed. The process itself was captivating, and a culture of collaboration across disparate areas of the firm was palpable.

Financial Engineering now produced prototypes that could be fed into the production queue. The bridge between product management and the researchers solidified from one of rope to beams.

The Twitter feed spilled over into sales and trading. Morning client communications exploited the apps generating the flow of information. A bridge of rope between the analytics folks and the traders appeared, which never existed previously. Steel reinforcement could come later.

The "question of the week" became an educational tool for the team. A consultant was tasked with developing a question and providing a half-page data-driven answer. People learned to write. Others had to read because the exercise was pushed directly out to the client base, generating questions. The trading desk pasted question and answer into morning client emails. They had to learn enough to respond when the clients reverted.

The ability of design thinking to change culture ought not to be surprising. Other corporate experiments reinforce this lesson. Pixar characterizes its workforce as a volunteer organization. On the Microsoft website, a lead sentence reads, "the Garage is a portal to hack culture at Microsoft." The last sentence of the paragraph says amazing synergies and connections across technologies and silos are made. Amen.

The winning of culture wars through design thinking is of interest beyond product and sales. We must pay a visit to Human Resources.

Chapter Notes

The letter upon which the title is based is one of several Bergman documents archived at Wesleyan University. The claim of Renoir's contribution to innovation culture is mine but seems obvious given timing of the letter and business history.

George Pólya's *How to Solve It* was his most successful work by commercial standards and remains in print since its first publication. I have never seen it referenced in the context of design thinking. The material on carrying out the plan is taken from his *Mathematical Discovery: On Understanding, Learning, and Teaching Problem Solving*.

In *A Study in Scarlet*, Sherlock Holmes lectures Dr. Watson on problem-solving. His most repeated lesson in later stories is derived from, "Most people, if you describe a train of events to them, will tell you what the result would be. ... There are few people however, who, if you told them a result, would be able to evolve from their own inner consciousness what the steps were which led up to the result. This power is what I mean when I talk of reasoning backward."

Kees Dorst is not a business guy but understands the need for clear definitions and a toolbox with which to implement them. He was on the Faculty of Design, Architecture, and Building at the University of Technology, Sidney, Australia, when he developed the concepts on which the what–how–value paradigm here is based. His work is academically dense, brilliant, and worth a look.

The Analytics Incubator won Wall Street's Mobile App of the Year award in 2016. The site boasted over 7,000 regular repeat visitors. This is a small number in social media terms, but the subsidiary's addressable market was only about 1,000 firms. A new corporate marketing regime was entrenching itself at the time. By the end of 2017, the Analytics Incubator was decommissioned as the firm refurbished its logo-branded toys. How this came about may be a story for another day.

CHAPTER 4

Minority Report

One of the great annual corporate events is the employee performance review. Its specific form differs across human resource departments, but the basic structure is common. Goals are set the preceding year. The employee writes a self-evaluation, and the manager may read it. A reply is tendered in the form of a combination of written and numerical scores. A face-to-face discussion is scheduled, and the appointment is sometimes kept.

Senior management insists the employee ranking system is for improvement and not for the purpose of compensation. Gaming is rife, because no one believes it. Software companies are happy churning out revisions to performance review software when users figure out the formats don't work very well. In turn, new formats lengthen the process each year as everyone (re)learns the system.

HR is built around the long term. Goal setting is a drip-down process starting somewhere near the top and flowing through the company's businesses and operational units. The process is a loser in companies evolving according to the principles of a gig economy. The first response is to institute more frequent performance reviews, even project by project. The goal is continuous mistake identification, course correction, and learning through iteration. Spot bonuses are the human equivalent of giving a dog a kibble for a lesson learned.

Peer-to-peer feedback re-emerges from a shadowy history of employee back-biting as teams become the employment unit, and their composition changes rapidly. The notion of a peer remains tied to seniority for the most part, however. A cultural atmosphere in which a junior person openly and without fear critiques someone quite senior is challenging. In one hedge fund where this practice is rampant, the hiring of senior members from outside the company is rare and often unsuccessful. The outsiders can never get used to it.

The Report Card

Compromises inherent in matching seniority with teams turned annual reviews into a public spectacle at my last firm. As many as 25 to 30 managing directors around the globe and across business units would gather in a virtual room to debate absolute and relative merits of an individual at a lower seniority rung. If a vice president was the subject, there might be a few directors in the room. Inclusiveness was the order of the day.

The philosophy was everyone should know what everyone else did around the company. Few of the evaluators knew the candidate. Fewer had a decent idea as to the individual's contributions to teams over the previous year. With so many involved, confidentiality associated with peer-to-peer comparisons disappeared. An 18-member executive committee evaluated managing directors, and the CEO dealt with the committee. A firm believer in the evaluation process, he did precisely that.

I received my annual review for which I had dutifully written a self-evaluation based on goals agreed the previous year. We discussed my comments and his input at length, and the CEO provided a written summary of conclusions.

Analytics, Inc. transition: Ian is to be commended for smoothly and rapidly transitioning his business to the global product organization. He cultivated strong leadership in [list of names] and identified a number of "rising talents" [list of names]. (Note to self: a good week's work followed by a long sigh.)

Promoting the brand as the high content thought leader and best in class analytics player: Ian had a productive year as a senior ambassador seeing clients, speaking at conferences, and attending advisory boards. He is sought out by a number of our key accounts. As Ian goes about his engagements, I would like to see Ian integrate his agenda more closely with regional leadership.

The Vice Chairman must parse corporate language.

"Integrate" means "change." Regional leadership comprises the CEOs of their respective geographical patches. Getting senior leaders to play nicely together is difficult, but critically important. The integration comment is a continuing theme, exposing the frailty involved in running a global operation through regional fiefdoms. The company was recovering from a legacy of local control, but old ways die hard. Back to the review.

> *Enhancing the company's capabilities and fostering a culture of innovation:* Ian has extensive experience evaluating execution performance. He worked with the portfolio trading function last year. I would like Ian to engage with execution desks to discuss performance challenges.

Engagement requires two parties. Lack of performance is not a message received well, hence the lack of current engagement. The report continued.

> Ian has gravitated to trying out new technology. He delivered several use cases with [technical jargon here]. Just as in the portfolio trading example, I would like to see Ian engage more closely with Product Management to identify opportunities for R&D which are in-line with operating priorities.

A sensible request, especially since my former research team of financial engineers was locked down to the point of not speaking to anyone under its new management. R&D here refers to the software technology department, however, and technology is not exactly my middle name. The relationship between technology and product management is complex, and a reorganization put the two under the same supervisory roof in order to push the strategic plan along. This is decidedly old-school, but we all tend to do things that worked once before. It is a cultural issue rather than a personal one. Culture was certainly on the CEO's mind:

> *Fostering/advocating culture change:* Ian effectively designed and launched "The Vice Chairman's Circle." Reviews have been mixed. This is not atypical of a new cross-functional, cross-seniority program. (Note to self: never teach another MBA course again.) I am not satisfied with our progress toward changing the culture; for example, breaking down historical silos, naturally collaborating

cross-region/cross-function, eliminating skepticism around strategy and plan, complacency, mediocrity, and lack of engagement with peers, driving urgency.

Chitchat is over, and we are finally talking. Here it comes.

Given Ian's experience, gravitas, and connectivity across the organization, he can be more impactful in fostering culture change. I would like to see him engage more closely with US Execution Management, global Product Management, Financial Engineering, and regional business and sales leaders to accelerate cultural transformation. Although partnership is a "two-way street," I'd like Ian to do more than his fair share to engage with these partners. Ian is an accessible leader.

OK! Desired culture is defined to be one of passion, discipline, commitment, and best operator in boilerplate review instructions. The Vice Chairman knows these characteristics are the products of a culture, not the fundamentals of cultural change.

Listen to the Stories

If you want to know about the culture, listen to the stories.

I thought the CEO might follow this advice and compiled several stories illustrating problem areas. The response was immediate: don't you believe in what we're doing here any longer? Never more, I replied, but the ensuing conversation was difficult. The philosophy seemed to be, if you want cultural change, change the stories.

If you want to change the culture, change the process. Better stories follow.

A leading example of this lesson is HR itself. The parent company had a dedicated HR staff with a leader who had grown up in very large organizations. Our processes stood up to those in any big corporation, but people and process remained overwhelmed by the reorganization, now two years old. There were dismissals to handle, recruitment to advance the multiyear strategic plan, onboarding, talent management, and new performance evaluation processes to develop, explain to the troops, and carry out. The staff broadcast the doctrine of passion, discipline, commitment, and best operator. They held contests promoting teams that embraced those values. Prizes were awarded.

HR was a topic in the packet of stories sent to the CEO. Here's how it goes.

The department had slipped away from the vanguard of cultural change. In fact, it was never there. Roles changed, but processes remained the same. Marketing was even given an HR badge to dress up the gospel, but the new doctrine was perceived to be much the same as the old doctrine, as well it may have been. The making of HR into apostles of values was not enough to create religion. To be fair, HR was never tasked with leading cultural change through investment in its own policies regarding employee engagement. They were busy and expended resources elsewhere.

Data on personnel and employee engagement were plentiful. Data management was an operational icon in the firm, and expertise in machine learning was available in several parts of the company. The industry knew us for our data analytics, but nowhere were these strengths brought to bear on change management. Data in HR manifested itself in compensation spreadsheets, records of occasional policy infractions, and annual review archives.

Time for some design thinking, I said. We must change the HR frame starting with employee engagement, a topic of multiple internal surveys with mediocre results and a likely enabler of broad cultural movement.

Social Engineering in the Corral of Law and Order

The business case for changing the extent and nature of employee engagement is well put by Diane Gherson, chief HR officer at IBM.[1] If people feel great about working with the company, clients will too. Supporting data are available: employee engagement numbers statistically explain two-thirds of client experience scores at IBM. An increase of client satisfaction by five points in an account delivers extra account revenue of 20 percent on average. The use of hard data to motivate change in the minds of management is a practical and political first step.

Value is engagement. Our existing frame was one of law and order.

Senior staff prescribed behavioral rules enforced through HR. The same was true for career development in terms of roles, promotions, and the like. Onboarding of personnel entailed orientation sessions and classes designed to be one size fits all. Learning and development were part of on-the-job training. The chore fell to localized operational management, and fragmentation of experience was the result. The practice reinforced the historical silos complained about by the CEO.

Change the frame to change the culture. Management provides a *how* that fits within the frame. The employees develop the *what* through experimentation, and the frame is the foundation of the laboratory. Replace the *how* as necessary.

Engagement is simultaneously personal and communal, and a sensible frame is social engineering.

Social engineering requires stimulus. Proctor and Gamble's approach, for example, was to build employees' capabilities and forge alternative relationships with managers to increase engagement. The company attempted to change managerial behavior from judging into coaching. There was investment in the managers' education with respect to proper feedback, alignment of aspirations with business needs, and employee learning plans. The process remained more drip down than direct when it came to the employees themselves, however. Stimulating management is a chore and not enough to get the job done.

The IBM experiments engineered by Diane Gherson and her coworkers are examples of cultural change through process. She credits experimentation through design reasoning with guidance, noting a fundamental shift in mindset was required. A change in mindset is another phrase for reframing.

IBM developed "concept cars" to test drive learning platforms and performance evaluation protocols. The *how* was a novel use of the Watson Analytics machine learning product. The platform was personalized to 380,000 individuals in an iterative fashion through consultation with employees.

Offerings are organized like a streaming service, and updates to the platform are motivated by employee ratings. A person's expertise is inferred from digital footprints inside the company, and personalized program recommendations are offered as stimulus to participate. Rewards and evaluations are handed out in the form of digital applied skills badges.

Ability to pinpoint capabilities drives adoption of data-based methodology in HR, and IBM claims skills inference by machine is 96 percent accurate. AI finds a use in talent acquisition at L'Oréal and

Hilton Hotels. Schneider Electric launched an AI platform for internal talent mobility, the Open Talent Market.[2] Management sees it as a career development exercise involving employee profiles and a range of jobs fitting skills and aspirations.

IBM's Checkpoint performance evaluation system gathered input from 100,000 employees. Stimulus was in the form of prototypes provoking employee reaction. Experimentation was possible once the social engineering frame was in place. Regular feedback from an employee-designed system, as opposed to managerial evaluations, was cited as the top reason employee engagement improved.

I concluded my story for the CEO with the observation that we relegated our machine learning applications to the design of algorithmic trading systems. Don't you believe in what we're doing here? Nevermore.

Culture in the Machine

The IBM experience suggests AI may enable change in business processes leading to new cultural principles. We must attend to machine learning's direct effects lest we risk becoming the ghost in the machine.

The First and Second Industrial Revolutions induced massive cultural change in nations subject to their influence. Industry was redesigned around physical capabilities of mechanization and electricity. Values shifted from agrarian principles to those developed by city dwellers engaging in the creation and implementation of new technology.

Industrialization tightened up moral codes through the alteration of practices interfering with productive labor. Life was work. The old morality was subsumed by the desire for an orderly society in which citizens would be submissive and industrious.

Industrial revolutions delivered nonagricultural jobs not involving skilled work, and the commoditization of labor led to unions as a form of communal protection. Cheap manufactured goods created a consumer culture, while steam engines for travel and the combination of telephone and telegraph introduced communication as a cultural norm. Long-distance communication was a natural consequence of the Second Industrial Revolution that brought electricity directly into our lives.

The Third Industrial Revolution entailed the use of electronics and digitization to automate production and modernize communication.

We are entering revolution number four according to consensus reached at the 2016 and 2020 World Economic Forums.[3] The upheaval is characterized by a fusion of technologies, which blurs lines between the physical, digital, and biological spheres. Welcome to Industry Version 4.0.

Organizations build business practices around collection and processing of data from across the company. IBM is only one example. American Express goes a step further by combining data on buyers with characteristics of sellers and vending information to both groups as well as to internal strategists. Algorithms are trained with input from departments from the back office to the operations and sales. A culture of secrecy is replaced by one of transparency.

Breaking down company silos will happen through process, because data can no longer be compartmentalized while serving multiple masters within the company. Human organization will follow suit in a setting within which traditional functional silos and boundaries can no longer exist.

The Machine Age witnessed a reconfiguration of society through the empowerment of machines with electricity. AI forces a culture shift, because it alters the relationship between data and humans as machines change from passive to active players in company life. The transformation may affect HR directly through skills that organizations seek and cultivate in employees, as illustrated by the IBM experience.

Hiring and promotion change character in the face of AI-induced culture. Candidate aptitude and workforce performance are measured in terms of analytical quality of thought and interactive abilities rather than basic knowledge and technical skills. Programmers may be the exception, but some believe even they will be replaced by machines that write their own code. Interviews assess empathy, emotional engagement, and lateral thinking, and such practice is a fundamental result of outsourcing to algorithms and their machines.

AI-induced culture manifests the paradox of automation, however. Manual workers required training to use machine tools during the Industrial Revolution. If you believe AI is only a business tool requiring retraining in how to expertly use it, prepare for unexpected events that appear ever more normal until a disaster occurs. As we increasingly rely on algorithms, we are less inclined to take control of exceptional cases when technology fails. If an automated system has an error, it will multiply the error until it is fixed or shut down. Digital enterprises become prone to systemic risk and are threatened by sensitivity to small changes requiring large responses. Large responses are costly.

If You Walk on Thin Ice, You Might as Well Dance

Design thinking as a candidate for process leading to cultural change is a natural in Industry 4.0. Some lessons and its affinity with AI are illustrated through a machine learning metaphor of a game. We are going to walk on water.

You face a frozen lake. The objective is to get to the other side. The lake is partitioned into a 4 × 4 grid, and you must take step one grid at a time, moving across or sideways. You earn a dollar if you make it but receive nothing for intermediate steps across the ice. If you step onto solid ice, refashion your strategy with the information and move again. Continue to add information in the form of your experience. A foot on weak ice sinks you; you die and are reincarnated at the edge of the lake. A breeze across the water may blow you from a step onto solid ice to a weak square, but you don't know anything about constantly changing wind speed or direction.

We don't know what to do. The *what* in this problem is a strategy for crossing the lake. Adopting a principle of random action as the *how* is a loser, and you already know this if you have been to a casino to play the slot machines. If not, you will die enough times in this game to finally figure it out. Value is represented by a dollar, but there are several steps and no contingent rewards. This microcosm of a world is one of imperfect information complicated by how the breeze blows.

A frame is reinforcement learning in which an agent corrects its movements every time it makes a mistake.[4] Reinforcement learning is a continuous process, and the principle becomes relative pricing within this frame. Although we have no contingent reward system, we choose a method that assigns value to each possible intermediate step given information available at the time a decision is made. Computing and allocating prices are time consuming, however, and it is freezing out here. A higher relative price for a block encourages us to step on a particular piece of ice. Every time we take a step, prices are adjusted.

This is called experimentation, and we are in Pólya's world of successive approximations.

Were this lake the company, process drives culture. It is one of problem-solving, continuous learning, and experimentation in the interest of discovering value. Contingent rewards are not part of the culture; rather, we compute the advantages of taking various steps and choose action based on an estimate of relative value in a world of imperfect information. We don't survive on immutable precepts. We frame problems for the purpose of discovering principles and ensuring survival.

Enlarge the pond to the size of Lake Michigan and the paradox of automation surfaces. Now there are millions of ice blocks. The algorithm is trained to calculate value for every possible combination of steps one might take. The number of computations is beyond imagination. The machine has none and tries anyway. The error is compounded the longer the machine runs on, and one of two things happen. Either the machine chokes on the problem and finally yields an undecipherable error message or more likely, it continues without end. None of us has time for a problem that takes a few thousand years to solve. A flashing red square with Error 420 doesn't help much either.

It's time for change in how we view the problem. The frame of learning remains appropriate, but the principle must change. An efficacious means of calculating value at each step is combined with a new algorithmic overlay, which approximates paths through another form of machine learning. Generic instructions for this sort of thing can be downloaded from Google in the form of the standalone TensorFlow or the packaged AI Platform. The entire process is about achieving maximum productivity with minimum wasted effort or expense. We can add efficiency to our list of cultural attributes.

A culture is created comprising problem-solving, continuous learning, experimentation, value creation, innovation, change management, persistence, and efficiency. Communicated and promoted by process, the players weave a cultural fabric that does not depend on motivational slogans.

In the Vice Chairman's preferred culture, no lake is too large.

Chapter Notes

The title is taken from Philip K. Dick's short story, although the Spielberg film starring Tom Cruise may be more recognizable. The central question is one of free will versus determinism. Ironically, themes include the role of media in a future state where technology make its presence virtually boundless. P.K. Dick is enjoying rediscovery through streaming services, and it is well deserved. He is a visionary.

A raw example of a firm with a challenge-culture is Bridgewater Associates. Ray Dalio's book, *Principles: Life and Work* provides a detailed blueprint of a no-holds-barred performance environment. It will scare you. Read it anyway.

The course mentioned in text was called *Leverage and Influence: What They Don't Teach in School.* I may never teach an MBA course again, but I did like my design of a class for vice presidents vying for directorship, and directors trying to scale the heights of a managing director. The problem in course preparation and delivery is always time, so I invited several guest lecturers whom I never did meet. Their TED Talks provided the basis of class discussion, and the modules went as follows. I list them, because everyone, absolutely everyone, should listen to these talks. Thank you, TED.com.

The Why, How, and What of the Company
> *Sim*on Sinek, The Golden Circle

Control is Not a Zero-Sum Game
> Itay Talgam, Lead Like the Great Conductors

The Cult of Great Ideas is Dangerous
> Linda Hill, How to Manage for Collective Creativity

Herding and Being Heard
> Julian Treasure, How to Speak So That People Want to Listen
> Adam Galinsky, How to Speak Up When You Feel You Can't

Getting in Gear
> Dan Pink, The Puzzle of Motivation

Design Thinking and the Language of Data
>Kenneth Cukier, Big Data is Better Data
>Manuel Lima, A Visual History of Human Knowledge

I recommend Diane Gherson's interview in Lisa Burrell's piece, "Co-Creating the Employee Experience," in *The New Rules of Talent Management*, Harvard Business Review, 2018. I unabashedly draw on the IBM experience in my discussion. Brilliant in many ways.

CHAPTER 5

Often Reality Is
Too Complex

Ron Suskind has a story to tell. His son was diagnosed with autism at the age of three. Owen stopped speaking.

Ron and his wife soon realized Owen had memorized every line from animated Disney movies, and Ron successfully communicated as the parrot Iago from *Aladdin*, using a puppet and speaking in Disney dialogue. Borrowing from the stories, tricks of this kind became a method to decode Owen's thoughts. Great progress was made as the couple identified themes, and the boy redefined sidekicks as the real heroes.

The moral of this tale about the power of stories is not in the culmination of the experience in the Oscar-nominated *Life Animated*. It is the boost to the use of passions as code breakers to understand autistic children's selves and the world. It is in the motivation for a collective of coaches, therapists, and doctors to participate in a machine learning app, fed remotely in the support of autistic personalities and their lives. It is about the influence of narrative.

The Vice Chairman adopts narrative as a discipline.

The discipline is consistency of use and the positioning of problems in the foreground of any story. Good tales have questions to answer while good answers support a more general narrative. A more general narrative provides a deeper foundation for influence. Storytelling is one of the sharpest implements in the leader's toolbox, but good knives can cut a finger as well as a bread.

Teller of Tales

Steve Jobs described the most powerful person in the world as the storyteller who sets the vision, values, and agenda. Great marketing is built around stories. If sales are the metric, the greatest line of all time may be shampoos' "rinse and repeat," but companies that tirelessly push messages out through repetition typically are not great marketers. If you want repetition, tell a story in a new way.

Originality is not required. Curating tales is good practice, and most audiences can be counted on to have never heard a particular one. You just need a purpose. Peter Gruber, the CEO of Mandalay Entertainment, reminds us purposeful storytelling isn't show business, it is good business.

The purpose of stories is the sale of ideas. If you heed this simple truism, there is no need to explore hundreds of references available on the art and form of storytelling. Edgar Allen Poe left behind a sufficient guide in three parts. Length must be short enough that the story is absorbed in a single sitting. The method of composition must be, well, methodical. Embellishments aside, good storytelling is an analytical business and not an off-hand response to a situation. It requires real work. Finally, craft the story only once you know how it will end. Stories have a goal, and the infusion of a story with the desired emotional response only comes with the ending in sight.

Storytelling is largely a verbal occupation in business. There are reasons for this, and some of them are poor. Multiple generations have passed through my shops, and most college graduates do not know how to write. Shame on us, but we can fix it. A more fundamental truth emerges when the focus turns to mature business types. People are afraid. Fear inhibits oral tradition and takes on a dangerous form with respect to the written word.

Writing commits a person to facts, opinions, and to the story. The act of writing implicitly assumes the story will be judged without the author being in the room. There is opportunity to parry criticism when we tell a tale directly to a crowd, but we are afraid to be pilloried without the chance of immediate redress, explanation, or escape when we write. Fear is a mind killer, and therein is a danger to any business enterprise or personal career.

Ray Dalio, chief of a successful hedge fund, nests the written word within personal interaction. A meeting at Bridgewater may begin in silence, and the silence attends the reading of a briefing document. The practice ensures all have read through the issues. Research and writing demand respect, and Dalio notes the importance of acknowledging the effort put into the work. There is a discipline inherent in writing a story down. Problems are clearly stated. Sentences have verbs, and paragraphs must begin with topical points. Stories should be brief and clear to be effective. The writer must face the fear but may defend ideas to the group.

Tell a Story to Control the Narrative

The idea and the emotion in any tale should be united. Conventional executive thinking is more of an intellectual process, but rhetoric is rarely inspiring. Stories resonate with the emotional part of our being, and culture is driven by emotion not logic. Never tell a tale describing how results meet expectations. Leave it to quarterly earnings reports. There is something much more important that needs doing.

The Vice Chairman controls the narrative.

Let's try an experiment. You have just been promoted to head of sales and have a set of organizational tasks to accomplish. A $25,000,000 book of business walks out the door. What are your first moves?

The question may seem silly, but similar situations occur frequently. In my example, the sales manager made two mistakes. He cast around for a quick turnover to an internal candidate for the job, which takes time. Then he delegated the client calls.

The manager lost complete control over the narrative by giving the departing salesperson a chance to first tell a story to the clients. The story is expensive to the firm whatever it may be. The error is compounded by delegating the company explanation and way forward to a junior person. Clients perceive this behavior as lack of respect.

Complete control of the narrative is sometimes aspirational, and practical alternative terminology might be to manage the story line. There is a trick to this—use stories to manage other narratives. Business types can learn something about narrative management by observing the political class at work.

A trivial example illustrates a general concept. Living in Chicago for a long spell, consistent exposure to Jesse Jackson was enforced through my partner's public sector work. It was frustrating to listen, because he rarely answered a question put to him directly. There was always a phrase to the effect: that's interesting and brings up the following point, whatever the point may have been. The phenomenon is not unique to Jackson. All politicians, and many outside the public sector, answer an easier question than the one posed. Nobel Laureates Daniel Kahneman and Amos Tversky demonstrate that most of us answer an easier question than the one originally asked.[1] There are alternatives to this obvious tactic, however, and a more recent political example illustrates.

By March of 2018, special counsel Robert Mueller had established a firm "no comment" policy in the minds of his staff and the public. In the same month, a headline in *POLITICO* read, "Mueller tight-lipped as media leaks shape Russia narrative." The conclusion was hardly surprising. Even late-night talk show hosts sculpted this story. The no-comment policy had created an informational vacuum.

Management of the narrative by another story was brilliant in its own way. The story? The special counsel is all about the facts. He cannot deny any one story without the risk that failure to respond to others would be interpreted as tacit confirmation. Real information is communicated through surprise and backed by action, because credibility is more important than the news of the day. The special counsel may reassess interactions with future witnesses, balancing the risk of leaks against information value. Control of the narrative remains in the special counsel's office.

The entertainment business also teaches lessons with respect to narrative management. We track the evolution of two tales, following basic principles of good story lines.

An event occurs. Shortly before the debut of a new reality show, a sex tape involving the star is released. Wow.

Already famous for being famous, Paris Hilton was blindsided. The tape was a development beyond her control: "I feel embarrassed and humiliated…never even thought these things would become public." Kim Kardashian was a woman without much in the way of public exposure at the time. She did a financial deal for her performance and turned the incident into content for the masses by making the tape an early plot point in her new TV show.

Expectations collide with reality. Even if the tape sold Hilton's own show, it was not part of her plan. She never owned the scandal nor redirected her narrative around it. A year later, she wrote that personal mystery was the key to fame. It was not, after the combination of early Trump-era exhibitionism and Girls-Gone-Wild beginning in the early 2000s. By contrast, Kardashian's expectations faced full frontal audience access to emotional nakedness. Whatever those expectations might have been, she turned every moment into carefully branded content. Sex was just part of the show.

What does the protagonist want in order to restore balance? This desire is a key component in storytelling. Paris Hilton used public appearances to further a brand while embracing mystery as part of a public relations strategy. Kim Kardashian promoted an illusion of 24/7 exposure in order to subordinate any one-time incident.

What is stopping the protagonist from attaining the desired outcome? Hilton wanted to be a conventional star, but convention of the Greta Garbo "I want to be alone" style didn't fit the new reality landscape. Kardashian is never alone.

Who are the antagonists? Every story needs a villain. For Paris, the antagonist is fame itself. She is unwilling to embrace the scandals of her own making. She believes in the power of mystery, and the conviction within killed her. Family drama provides all the antagonists required by Kim, who stages fights for content. Lovers are married in lavish ceremonies and rejected shortly afterward, all for the creation of antagonists to further personal narrative.

The lesson? Paris lost the publicity battle to the point of appearing to be a Kardashian lackey. By Instagram standards, her 8.5 million followers pale in comparison to Kim's 100+ million. The story illustrates the consequences of complete misunderstanding contrasted with an appreciation of situational context. Different lessons can be taught based on the various choices made by people under pressure. Paris Hilton truly believed in her personal narrative, which brings us to the difficult issue of truth in storytelling.

Truth Is a Relative Concept

Film director Jean Luc Godard said, "Sometimes reality is too complex. Stories give it form." This is nowhere more true than in the phenomenon of confabulation.

In the 15th century, confabulation meant "a talking together, chatting, familiar talk." The meaning comes from *fabulari*, to talk or chat, which in turn stems from *fabula*, a tale. Talking in stories sounds great and consistent with the cutting power of narrative. Confabulation is about the knife slicing a finger.

Confabulation is the telling of a story that is fictional, while the teller believes it is true. The storyteller has no intention to deceive, but there is a striking mismatch between what a person means to do (tell a true story) and what the person does (fiction). Confabulation is most often discussed in the context of mental illness but is a common occurrence and prevalent in the workplace. People make stuff up and are not aware.

We confabulate to make sense of experience, perceptions, and feelings, and sometimes because we are driven to infer causality. There is a complementary body of scientific evidence on memory suggesting memories are constructs and the construction is a mix of fact and fiction.[2]

Even if we are not predisposed to act in this manner, we do it when pushed. Researchers laid out a range of items such as pairs of socks in one experiment and asked subjects to select one.[3] Participants consistently preferred items on the most right-hand side. When questioned to explain the choices, they did not mention the position of the items even when displayed pairs of socks were identical. They instead attributed the choices to texture or color. Not knowing the factors causing the selection, the subjects produced explanations not based on evidence, rather on plausibility. Confabulation.

Traders do this all the time. There is always a story as to why a trade went bad, but the tale may not coincide with the hard data. Those data are discounted in favor of the story, and the greater the evidence, the harder the pushback. The traders are not lying; they believe. The trade happened before the data appeared, and something fills the gap if the knowledge is not immediately available. Once filled, we tend to believe and thereby deny further evidence.

Godard is almost correct. Reality is too complex, not just sometimes, and confabulation is a result. There are many explanations of confabulation and even some experimental studies, but a simple rationale is appealing.[4] We cannot hold enough information to find the order in chaos. We nevertheless construct order through stories.

Shortly after Dr. Watson met Sherlock Holmes, he attempted to explain the Copernican theory of the universe to the detective. Holmes responded he would do his best to forget it. The reason? Only a fool fills the empty attic of the brain with lumber of every sort, crowding out useful knowledge, or at best jumbling it with irrelevancies. It is a mistake, he says, to think the little room of a brain has elastic walls and can distend to any extent.

Lest you deny wisdom in the form of old fiction, consider the findings of the neuroscientist, Morten Kringelbach.[5] He concludes we simply do not have access to all the unconscious information on which we base decisions. We create fictions upon which to rationalize them. We cannot hold so much information in our consciousness, and if we stopped to think about how we made every choice, we might not get anything done. One of the creators of the socks experiment, Timothy Wilson, claims our senses may take in more than 11 million pieces of information each second. The most liberal estimates suggest we are conscious of only 40 of them.

The Vice Chairman is aware of confabulation and must deal with its consequences. The advice also applies to the personal brand. You may have a high confabulation score. Get tested by a psychologist. My score is low, but the claim is not confabulation. Just a fib, not a fabula.

People with paralyzed limbs or even blindness may deny they have anything wrong with them, if only in the short term. The analog in business is common. Give an important job to a busy person, as the saying goes. How many times have you heard a manager say, I'm overwhelmed? This may not be whining or work avoidance, and often, it is simply true. If you have been in a position to hear this, you observed another common phenomenon: offer additional responsibilities to the overwhelmed, and they willingly, even avidly, accept. They do not have the bandwidth to handle the job and fail not only with respect to the new role but also in the fulfillment of old tasks. They confabulate, and the result is harmful to themselves and the firm. Human Resources take note: effective goal setting is not a check-the-box or "stretch" exercise and is more complicated than one might think.

Confabulation compromises understanding of reality and of ourselves. On a positive note, behavior driven by factors unknown to us can be integrated into a wider belief system and sense of value. We call this identity, and it is the foundation of a brand in the marketplace. Failures due to confabulation originate in pure acceptance and the accompanying lack of desire to bring data to a problem. This acceptance may be unknowing in and of itself.

Stories by Design

Design thinking provides a static framework and a dynamic process for the telling of tales. A problem is in the foreground by definition, and the framework mitigates confabulation by creating a testable set of conclusions. Common language develops within a team and contributes to a culture of problem-solving. We resonate to a process with clearly enunciated steps. Storytelling via design reasoning yields culture through a well-defined process manifested through common language and its use. It is a language of innovation.

Value is the hero, and all heroes need description. Value should align with the firm's means of value assessment and must be specific in any story. Telling management "data science will improve process thereby adding value" is a loser. The easiest value assessments involve cost, making cost the antagonist. Enunciate cost in terms of time translated into money. Cash always gets attention.

Stories based on design reasoning are simple in two cases and impossible in another. The last is when value is unknown, in which case there is no useful story to tell. If principles of *how* are known, the tale is descriptive. *What* should be produced is described, and how it adds value is explained. If the storyteller is selling a new principle for the production of an existing product, the process is equally simple and obvious.

The interesting case parallels the more difficult design problem in which the *how* and the *what* are unknown. The storyteller knows the solution and is trying to communicate. The audience does not know what product is envisioned or the means by which it is to be produced. An example illustrates.

An institutional brokerage monitors the algorithmic trading of hundreds of orders each day. Efficiency is paramount, but current practice requires multiple computer screens per trader, many traders, and manual shifting between orders to update information. Failure to keep track of even a single order can damage client returns. The loss of a client generates additional expense through the search for new clients to maintain revenue. Automation of data analysis and visualization reduce the number of traders required per hundred orders, the number of screens needed as capital, and client loss through better information. Savings are estimated in the gazillions.

The *what* and *how* may be clear to the innovator, but they are not clear to the company. Treat them as unknowns. If there is uncertainty about the product and current working principles do not apply, the audience believes the single equation cannot be solved. The storyteller must provide a frame to connect *how* to *value* and thereby develop the principle underlying the production of *what*.

The frame in use is high touch trading in which many traders are needed to provide personalized service. Each trader specializes in a narrow set of stocks. Information is stored in the trader's head and not shared in the interest of job preservation. Traders do their own market research but ignore potentially useful information beyond their immediate purview because they cannot keep track of all the correlations involved. High touch traders nevertheless are paid gobs of money.

A different frame is introduced:

A new frame is low touch trading. The old frame relies on depth of information more suitable for identifying longer run investment returns, but an institutional client already has made those decisions. The information required in the new frame need be sufficient only for the efficient execution of orders. Quality of execution, measured in terms of frictional costs of trading in the market, is the benchmark by which clients judge traders in an electronic world. Giving the client some control over strategy selection and order execution lowers the service level but is desired by the client base. The clients search for efficient implementation of their investment decisions at low cost.

Once a frame is in place, design thinking is nothing more than IF-THEN statements. The frame connects a principle of production, the *how*, to *value*. IF we use principle X, THEN we produce Y to generate value.

Low touch trading fundamentally consists of shipping and monitoring. Orders are shipped in, allocated to algorithms, and monitored over their life span in the market. Results are shipped back to the client. Shipping already is part of the firm's infrastructure. A principle of monitoring is telemetry: IF telemetry is a principle of efficient trading in a low touch world, THEN build sensors and an alert mechanism. The expected path of the algorithm's executions is compared against actual executions in real time. The sensors send signals to traders only when actual results deviate in a negative fashion from those expected. Trader time is expended only when necessary, saving gazillions of dollars.

The story may end at this point but also may be extended to include the results of experimentation. Completed equations must be tested, and prototypes are helpful.

The storyteller might engage in simple projects that can be finished in a short period of time. People forget the point of the story, and attention spans are short. A physical representation need only confirm appropriateness of the principle and the value added. If an experiment is to be added to the storyline, the prototype should be tangible and actionable.

A dashboard will consume about two weeks of a single person's work. Speed comes from ignoring the shipping problem and deliberate omission of the allocation of orders to strategies implemented through the firm's algorithms. Nevertheless, the prototype will be complete enough to show to clients.

Design thinking demands client feedback and also makes it possible to extend story lines. What is missing in the tale? Reexamine the assumptions.

IF proper allocation of orders to trading strategies is a principle of efficient trading in a low touch world, THEN build a database and a clustering algorithm to sort thousands of stocks into clusters based on trading performance by strategy.

Communication is achieved through frames to model the firm, a problem and value of its solution, and testable conclusions.

The story leads with the problem. It avoids confabulation by demanding experimentation. *What + How = Value* is the basis of a practical language. Storytelling via design reasoning yields culture through process:

IF design thinking is a principle of communication in the frame of selling ideas, THEN tell a story by design to create understanding.

All Things Are Metaphors

A common framework for stories does not stifle creativity of expression. Telemetry, for example, is a metaphor for a process that may take on physical, digital, or transcendental form. Creativity through metaphor is a common sport.

I relied on Sherlock Holmes' description of crowding out useful knowledge with useless attic lumber in the discussion of information overload. We still understand it today, but the image is more 19th than 21st century. Hasan Minhaj provides a Millennial twist with the brain as a browser filled with too many open windows and recommends closing a few to make meaningful connections. Holmes and Minaj create a familiar association to describe a complex neurological phenomenon. Familiarity depends on situational context, including the age of the audience. Sherlock Holmes and Hasan Minaj are connoisseurs of metaphor.

The concept has intrigued us for thousands of years. According to Aristotle, the greatest thing by far is to be a master of metaphor; one cannot learn it from others. Einstein talked of trains and clocks, then wove time and space into a single fabric. See, it's not so hard. We do it all the time.

The Vice Chairman uses metaphor as a way of thought before it is a way with words.

Metaphor is the capacity to perceive a resemblance between elements from separate domains or areas of experience. Only then can they be linked together in linguistic form. The poet Robert Frost wrote, an idea is a feat of association and the height of it is a good metaphor. Unless you are educated in metaphor, he thought you are not safe to be let loose in the world. Frost has a point. Metaphors are not only components of stories. They are mini stories in and of themselves. Like stories, metaphor has dangers as well as benefits.

Many business types pride themselves on "connecting the dots." Metaphor structures the dots and organizes the connections. Coherent explanations emerge. As an interpersonal device, use of metaphor injects an emotional effect into an otherwise logical argument. Metaphor showcases some dots and shapes the way people act.

Metaphor also is employed to hid some of those dots from public view. Those who do so understand its usage well. While metaphor reflects historical reality, it also plays a role in constructing a new one. This is sometimes called ideological behavior, and such behavior crowds out the problem-solving benefits of using metaphor in the first place, somewhat like confabulation.

John J. Clancy categorizes popular use of metaphors in business. They are journey, games, war, machine, organism, and society.[6]

Each category on the top of Table 5.1 is the basis for a metaphor, while those arranged on the vertical are illustrations of points we want to get across. A journey entails goals, difficulty, and risk. Journeys are unpredictable, require leadership, and rarely succeed without cooperation. The activity of organisms provides metaphor describing culture, risk of survival, and complex reactions to situational context. Society speaks to common goals and illustrates cultural behavior together with community

Table 5.1 Use of Metaphor in Business

	Journey	Game	War	Machine	Organism	Society
Goal	X	X	X	X	X	
Difficulty	X	X	X			
Risk	X		X		X	
Leadership	X		X			X
Predictability	X	X		X		
Strategy		X	X			
Complexity			X	X		
Purpose	X	X	X		X	
Teamwork	X	X	X	X		
Culture					X	X

leadership. You may fill in the matrix differently than I or add talking points as they arise. It is your story after all.

Why bother with a list of the most popular metaphors? The answer is familiarity. People need a connection with a potentially strange concept when trying to comprehend an explanation that itself requires a metaphor for understanding. I learned this lesson from one of my chief financial officers who often said he couldn't make sense of my analogies, which I had deliberately made original in and of themselves. A shift to the familiar made for easier digestion in board and executive committee meetings.

Like stories, metaphor construction should be methodical in business settings, and this can be difficult. A student of metaphor, James Geary, claims we utter about six of them a minute.[7] The large number implies they are brief on average but hardly analytical. If there is a single ending to each of the six, repetition is the only result.

Too many of these devices becomes ridiculous. Expositors walk a narrow path between too much and just enough. A newspaper writing coach put forward a simple guideline: if your audience starts noticing cause more than consequence, it is probably too much.[8] Try structuring your metaphors according to design thinking principles: IF something is true, THEN the concept is realized as value in some form or fashion.

Perception, Comprehension, and
the Event Horizon

The Vice Chairman interrogates stories.

The discipline of narrative suggests we question explanations in the form of tales. The practice helps avoid pure acceptance and guards against confabulation. A case in point is situational awareness and the ability to put a business problem in context. Two metaphors illustrate.

In the movie, *Batman Begins*, our hero is counseled by his mentor to always be aware of the immediate surroundings. The villain-to-be makes the point by cracking surrounding ice, just as Batman thinks he is making a killing blow. The hero plunges into the icy water, triumph extinguished.

A Swedish company, Facit, once made the finest mechanical calculators in the world. The belief in superiority of product crowded out awareness of the revolution in electronic devices. Confabulation was evident. The engineers began to check the mechanicals for accuracy with cheap electronic calculators. Within six months, the company went from record revenues to disappearance. Icy water, indeed.

A dictionary definition of situational awareness is wordy enough to confuse. Environment effects, space, time, perception, and future projections are words found therein. Most plainly, situational awareness is an understanding of the environment within which we make decisions. Key descriptors include context, circumstance, and consequences.

A leader begins with context. The word encompasses forces shaping the business environment and decision making within it. Paris Hilton failed here while Kim Kardashian succeeded.

Circumstance comprises the situation as it unfolds dynamically. The critical question is, what is changing? Consideration of circumstance dominates thinking in product management in which evolving competition and future market conditions are essential lines of inquiry. Product launch dates and success are dependent on a forecast of circumstance in a world of imperfect information.

There is a laudable move to push decision making to those on the factory floor. Those people need to be aware as well. Continuing educational requirements typically miss this bit, which brings us again to confabulation.

Any team leader depends on updates and progress reports from the field. Confabulation in this context means the description of the situation may only be a partial representation of the truth. Some evidence is shed due to crisis, and other evidence may be lost because there is too much information. The leader's situational awareness takes a hit as the result. Listen with a skeptical ear. Start asking questions and don't be confrontational. The team doesn't know individuals are confabulating.

As in the socks experiment, explanations may be produced not based on evidence, rather on plausibility. Given a choice between credibility and truth, credibility wins almost every time. This part of human nature opens the door to confabulation in the workplace.

A good problem-solver guards against confabulation while maintaining credibility. Does new information render a potential solution more credible? Is the information a sign of increasing proximity to a solution? If the answer is no to the latter, and yes to the former, it's time to move on. And so, we will.

Chapter Notes

Ron Suskind is a Pulitzer Prize-winning author and interviewer of the politically famous. He talks of searching the world for spellbinders which can be retold but tells pretty good tales on his own.

The Edgar Allen Poe reference is to an essay entitled, "The Philosophy of Composition." If you are a fan of the poem, The Raven, it is a must-read. If not, read it anyway.

The formulaic style of identifying imbalance with an antagonist and casting the protagonist as the entity destined to restore balance is well expressed for business applications in "Storytelling That Moves People," *Harvard Business Review*, June 2003.

Yes, Girls Gone Wild was a real show. #MeToo.

The snippet by Sherlock Holmes is from *A Study in Scarlet* by Arthur Conan Doyle.

"All things are metaphors" is attributed to Johann Wolfgang von Goethe. There are many definitions of metaphor, and the one used here relies on Howard Gardner, who in turn gives credit to traditions dating back to ancient Greek philosophy.

I owe the example of Facit calculators to a TED Talk by Knut Haanaes entitled, *Two Reasons Companies Fail—and How to Avoid Them.*

CHAPTER 6

New Vocabulary for the New Normal

Still talking about the "new normal?" Forget it. The term du jour is *normalization of deviance*, by which unexpected and risky events appear as ever more normal—until a disaster occurs. Insensitivity grows over time because disaster often does not happen until other critical factors align. We can thank analyses of the Challenger and Columbia space shuttle failures for the wording, but it is just the beginning of novel terminology applied to markets and corporate life.

New language brings new definitions, and definitions change the topology of influence. They constitute the foundation of government and corporate policy. Language is the life blood of stories, and its emotional trappings are channels through which we change culture.

The financial crisis of 2008 reintroduced *systemic risk* as the risk of collapse of an entire financial system. Systemic risk also refers to the collapse of any market, and there is a natural extension to industries. The Flash Crash of 2010 brought the idea to center stage in discussions of trading market structure. Blackrock characterized the driver of the early 2018 market sell-off as a set of financial products that could "blow up the industry."

Once industry participants exhausted detailed and commonplace terms such as circuit breakers and stop-loss orders, policy makers searched for new language to describe the issues at a higher level. The new vocabulary applies equally well to corporations. Internal workings of a company exhibit the same characteristics as any market.

Stability in Companies and Markets

A key concept is stability. Systemic stability is threatened by *nonlinearities* in market and corporate responses. Digital environments are sensitive to small changes resulting in large responses, and this perspective permits the entrance of terms such as *contagion and path dependence*. A reemergence of *chaos theory* seems inevitable. It all sounds frightening, even when a dictionary is consulted; that is part of the point.

Closely linked to stability are the role of information and changes in its structure. Small differences in signal relative to noise can have disproportionate changes in outcome. A leading example prior to computerization of markets is bank runs, suggesting an old idea reborn. *Fake news* as noisy signal fits into this category.

Newer is the incursion of game-theoretic theories of information into debates over issues such as fragmentation of company functions. A common mantra is "knock down the silos." It is argued, for example, that technology has removed *common knowledge* from divisions, possibly from individual employees, and certainly from markets.

You may think common knowledge means everyone knows about an event. If so, revamping of priorities should be doing its job along with the news. Priorities are repriced and reordered accordingly. But, no … even if all participants know the status of the event, prices will not adjust completely. Everyone knows about the event status, but there can be participants who do not know that others know. The result is severance of the link between corporate priorities and valuation. The beliefs replacing said link include a willingness to believe in the concept of common knowledge itself. Brace yourself: senior management may well do so, and reorganization is a common result.

The Vice Chairman does not accept new terms based on common interpretations. A fresh dictionary is required, and it is a responsibility to build the dictionary as a living document. An ongoing written review of competitors' strengths, activities, and scope is a useful analogy.

Nonlinear response and information effects flow together in the introduction of *endogenous risk* to the lexicon. The term is used to identify characteristics nested within market and corporate structures leading to mutual and pernicious feedback loops, regardless of rational behavior.

Also pernicious is the use of such editorial language as part of a fear factor being hardwired into the environment, just as feedback itself is said to be hardwired into the computerized system. As more decisions are taken by robot systems, the higher the risk of wild feedback loops within the company. Welcome to *machine learning*.

Twisted

Several twists and turns are on the table. *Risk feedback loops* underlying financial crises are repurposed to describe agile computer programming protocols that elevate failure by construction. Newly imposed risk limits lead to inventory reduction, depressing prices and thereby increasing and risk and potential loss. Value destruction spills over into finance, which withdraws from its intermediation role, affecting the larger company. Contagion.

The connection between liquidity and valuation leads to *shallowness feedback loops*. Volatility of operations rises with growth; corporate liquidity declines; and the distribution of analyst recommendations becomes more disperse. Small signals then generate large moves in the market reference price feeding back into more data dispersion. Contagion now comes together with *cascades*. Political events have been described by the term to an extent illustrated by over 673,000 references tying cascades together with Nancy Pelosi's name alone.

Closely related to shallowness, digital analytics nourish *news feedback loops*. News feedback once was fueled by pigeons returning from the battlefield with information, an improvement in technology relative to the king's horses. Digital news effects now join the party. Tactical corporate data are picked up through the medium and reinforce directional price movements, distorting value. The failure of price discovery and value creation follows. How much is the company worth, anyway?

Delay feedback was introduced to the public by financial markets' belated price reporting behavior in the crash of 1987. The term is recast in market and corporate settings in which delay is linked to the interplay between fragmentation and falling markets. Congestion leads to time lags, and lags turn into mispricing at market centers. Computers sell into declines, and the delay feedback amplifies *price feedback loops*.

Delay feedback is the bane of corporate product management. Feedback is forged from the interplay between prioritization of individual product development and fragmented technical skills, leading to congestion. Cascades characterize failing schedules.

Fallacies of Composition

Of interest to management should be *index feedback loops*. In financial markets, as volatility rises, single-stock swings increase, and factors are mispriced. The market for exchange-traded funds (ETFs) then suffers from illiquidity, leading to a reduction in the linkage between the ETFs and baskets of stocks. Market making in the individual securities is affected, and more mispricing results. ETFs may eventually hit rock bottom.

Index feedback loops stem from two sources within a corporate environment, consolidation of business lines and the bundling of goods and services in sales. The former is a result of diversification into areas exhibiting complementarities. The latter is exploitation of complementarities in the sales process. The term, *solution sales* becomes a mantra.

Revenue in a bundled operation is simple summation, but profitability creates implicit index weights through the allocation of cost synergies. Allocation methodology lacks standardization regardless of industry. Differing price multiples across bundled activities inject an index mindset into company valuation.

As competitive pressures shift and suppliers' costs change, the volatility of component contributions increases. Company factors are mispriced, leading to a break in the link between those components and the value of the firm. Divestiture is a common consequence. Individual components affect bundled sales, exacerbating the phenomenon. Diversification leads to a lack of stability, and we are back to systemic risk.

Calls in Europe and the United States for submission of computerized trading software to national authorities for review reflect systemic concerns. At a micro level, company policies regarding integrity of new computer code are written. Between the lines of the new lexicon, both efforts are found to be useless. *The fallacy of composition* suggests the digital enterprise can be unstable even if every computer algorithm looks good.

The fallacy of composition is applicable to organizational and product structure within a corporation. Every division may do well while sacrificing a company's global growth. Synergies can be negative as well as positive. Individual products may garner revenue gains, while profits lag due to lack of efficient cross-subsidization. Keep the fallacy handy at your next board meeting.

We now characterize companies and markets as *socio-technical system-of-systems*. The market is composed of interconnected constituents, each of which is an independent system with no single coordination point. The old example was the foreign exchange market; a new one is securities market trading structure, reflected in the furor over meme stocks. The newest is the corporation-as-digital-enterprise.

There is a natural coordination point in companies, at least where things meet at the top. Integration of logically independent systems nevertheless remains problematic, however. The terminology is depressing for those interested in predictions regarding stability and systemic risk. Little established science permits an understanding of how to control these systems, because they are so different from those studied in the past. The term becomes the full-employment act for systems researchers as the idea gains traction. In the meantime, it sounds impressive but could use a little rebranding at the level of senior management and boards of directors.

#inventwordsbeforetheyinventyou

Managers should pay attention to invention of language used by employees. Boomers may be the last to study *neologism* in school, because the creation of new words is simply a day-to-day occurrence today. The term also means a word understood only by the speaker and derives from the study of schizophrenia. Novel word creation creates its own normalization of deviance. Confabulation may be the result.

The best defense against linguistic onslaught is to invent your own words. The terms do not have to be original; *repurposing* will do. General Motors elevated repurposing to a new level in 2018 when they referred to the closure of five plants with a loss of 14,000 jobs as being *unallocated*.

Business word invention can be elevated beyond obscure jargon to the art of explaining entire strategies through a single term. Done right, it explains or justifies personal and corporate brand positioning. Rebranding may be old news, but *reintermediation* and *rebundling* fit the description as examples.

Disintermediation occurs when an intermediary is forced out due to structural change. The Internet browser's thesaurus refused a synonym and asked me whether I really meant disintegration suggesting lack of common usage. Brick-and-mortar retailers face disintermediation through online shopping. Portfolio managers encounter disintermediation through robo-investing. The response is to *reintermediate*. Reintermediation is the process by which a disintermediated entity is re-established in the new environment. Retailers and brokers face the unbundling of functions performed as well or better by *reintermediaries*. Brokers and retailers alike move to *rebundle*, motivated by a search for opportunities that might aid in the process of survival.

Reintermediation through rebundling depends on creative combinations of product and service elements leveraging technology and information in novel ways. The academic world arguably introduced rebundling in the late 1990s in the context of brokers and securities exchanges.[1] Industry prophets reinvented the term in 2015 in the context of banking services. The first 20 or so hits on rebundling in an Internet search now yield the use of the term in education, fintech, music, film, and financial services. These reinventions all are dated 2018 to 2020. Some things take time, but rebundling as a process has taken on the extra chore of *rebranding*.

The Vice Chairman maintains a sense of humor in a world of normalized deviance. In fact, this whole chapter is a *mashup*, a musical term repurposed to mean a combination of any two things that do not, on the face of either one, belong together. The *electronic mail game* adds to the fun, by making disparate market outcomes depend on what each trader believes any other trader believes about yet any other traders' beliefs about all other traders, and … you get the picture. Some once called this the art of picking stocks. Substitute "competitor" for "trader" and you have the art of strategic management.

Chapter Notes

Normalization of deviance was introduced by sociologist Diane Vaughan when studying the Challenger disaster. She identified the root cause of the Challenger explosion as being related to the repeated choice of NASA officials to fly the space shuttle despite a dangerous design flaw.

The reference to index feedback loops owes its existence to the Flash Crash of May 2010. Much has been written about this event. Supposedly it was the failure of computerized market making that reduced the natural single stock to ETF relationship. One indicts the financial product, the market structure, and a single class of participants for systemic risk in one pass, a perfect hat-trick in policy circles. In hindsight, the truth is somewhat different, and I recommend "The Flash Crash *Is* History," in the June 2010 issue of *Advanced Trading*.

CHAPTER 7

Marriage Is a Corporation

TED Talks are sometimes funny, often provocative, and usually entertaining. One day, when I was thinking about marriage, TED.com seemed a natural place to look. I was feeling for a pulse away from academics on the one hand, social media distortion on the other, and divorce pundits in between.

Nothing. Well, almost nothing. Marriage is not a *topic* for over 2,600 TED listings. A search of the site reveals pages of titles not associated with the concept as search engines are prone to do when they cannot find anything.

Marriage is one of the most important social and cultural institutions on the planet. Tribes of all sorts go to war over it. Religious schisms develop. Annualized marriage rates in OECD countries may be falling in recent history but still hover at five per 1,000 people, and we are talking about billions of people. In the United States alone, we see 2.1 million marriages a year. Yet, the only direct hit on the topic was a light-hearted account by Jenna McCarthy, an independent TEDx Talk for which speakers are not chosen by the TED editors. Her advice? Don't win an Oscar for best actor.

Do not giggle or snort. The Oscar marriage curse is a feature of Hollywood history and is just as real in corporations. I have watched friends, who made it into those *Forty Under Forty* lists, get sidelined within a year of the entrance of new senior management.

Marriage has something to say with respect to corporate operation and governance. These teachings range from team interactions to bigger pictures of corporate activity.

The Urge to Merge

Why do we start down the seemingly disparate roads of marriage and corporation? McCarthy reminds us there are hundreds of legal benefits to being married, gained from the government. Why do corporations exist? Legal benefits. Those prizes may be necessary to maintain a relationship, but they are not sufficient.

Statistics tell us 50 percent of marriages end in divorce within a decade, and the failure rate of mergers and acquisitions sits somewhere between 53 and 70 percent. Less formal partnerships, put together to provide comprehensive product to a consumer set, are increasingly popular. They are fundamental building blocks of the gig economy as well. The better these are papered to resemble merger, the more likely to fail in my experience.

The language used by survey designers in order to explain splits in marriages and corporations unnaturally varies. A side-by-side comparison in Table 7.1 is easy to interpret, however.

Table 7.1 Failure in marriage and companies

Divorce	Merger failure
Lack of commitment	Lack of line management involvement
Argue too much	Inability to integrate effectively
Infidelity	Misunderstanding of value propositions
Unrealistic expectations	Inadequate due diligence
Lack of equality	Ignoring cultural differences and synergies
Lack of preparation for marriage	False sense of security prior to merger
Love over experience	Hope over experience

The last comparison is mine, but the remainder merit 40 to 70 percent of mention by respondents in various surveys.

Marriage is a process of evolving cultural fit. Achievement of cultural accommodation in companies is the most difficult hurdle to clear in the world of mergers and partnerships. Ways in which marriages achieve such a goal are instructive in the matter of corporate affairs beyond the issue of mergers.

Love is grand, but the key to a long-running relationship is being a good roommate. Failure to act in this manner is the grist of TV sitcoms. They last only half an hour and always end well. Not so in real life. Failure to properly shape the squeezing of a toothpaste tube may be funny in *Friends*, but hair on the communal soap bar is grounds for static in the household. There is a reason directors insert static into movie scenes: they are trying to make you uncomfortable. We tend to move away from discomfort.

Unintended consequences rule in poor roommate conditions. Being a good cook goes a long way until uncleaned grease on the floor becomes a continuing irritant to the other party. The corporate world doesn't deal well with unintended consequences regardless of origin.

Do you tell your companion every time you do something for the household? I hope not, for your sake. When was the last time you did something for someone in the company without disturbing your peers or running to the boss? If you must pause, you have not fostered integration within the firm.

The inability to integrate effectively ranks as the most critical corporate item of concern in Deloitte studies.[1] Successful integration is a social contract, and this is true for teams, company initiatives, and merger activity alike. Marriage has something to say about such agreements.

Contracts Are Not Holy Relics

When I married, the two of us had arrived at a stage where statistics predicted a 73 percent chance of failure. We represented a bad fit in almost every conceivable way, and the situation remained so for over 35 years. But we both believed marriage is a contract, and not just the one signed on a wedding day. Roles, responsibilities, and lines not to be crossed. Verbal, short, and explicit. The details are unimportant and undoubtedly idiosyncratic.

What *was* important is one restriction: neither party could mention the word *divorce* or walk out in the middle of a year, and the agreement could only be changed annually. While some go out for an anniversary celebration, we had dinner for the purpose of renegotiating the contract.

When her children finally realized what was going on, they demanded discontinuation of the practice. So much for setting examples.

A key to this contractual arrangement is a belief contingent motivators often do not work. Think of a contingent motivator as a prize: if one accomplishes a task within certain guidelines, there is a reward. The motivation suffices for a simple set of rules and a fixed goal. Marriages don't function as such. Attempts to mimic human problem solving with AI cum deep learning algorithms don't even work this way; there is no reward for an intermediate step, and one obtains the prize only at the end of the game. Tactical moves lead to a reset of strategy at every major step in the process. Renegotiation.

Rules are rarely simple in a company setting. Fixed goals are scarce in successful enterprises because companies are too busy adapting to environmental pressures to care about them. Scientific studies suggest prizes are ineffective in problems that require discrimination in perceptions of functionality. A company may chart a clear destination for the sake of its stakeholders, but the typical enterprise still offers rewards for intermediate steps.

Why do most companies have social contracts in place depending on contingent motivators? Management faces three seemingly unsolvable problems possessing solutions worked out by married couples.

The Problem With Excellence

Excellence is preached as a cultural beacon, and mastery of one's craft is an essential chapter in any behavioral bible. Excellence is quickly generalized to *best*, generating the first problem. Best at what you do, best in the business, best product, a company that simultaneously embodies organizational excellence, optimally efficient operation, and creative innovation. Whatever.

The concept of optimality doesn't exist in sophisticated learning and operational methodology. Great designers tell you *best* is beyond theoretical and incremental improvements rule. Good product comes from matching frames of reference to behavioral principles, an experimental process with no best in sight. On the other hand, contingent motivation is designed to reward this generalization of excellence. The reward cannot be right if the motivation is wrong.

The notion of incremental may be self-referential and thus derided as being noncompetitive if not lazy. Use the term, *better*, if it makes you more comfortable. You may not need to be the best, but you do need to be better than the others. McCarthy says the woman doesn't have to be thin, just thinner than her partner in the happiest of marriages. Best companion is the stuff of romantic comedies, and she advises against watching such shows with a spouse.

In marriage, this line of thought leads to the *good enough relationship*. *Good enough* is pejorative in the workplace. This reflects a misunderstanding of the term.

Relationship guru John Gottman says some people believe happiness in a relationship requires lowering their expectations to avoid disappointment. This, he opines, is a bad idea. When you lower your expectations, you are more likely to settle for being treated poorly.

Couples in a good enough relationship settle for nothing less than being treated with honesty, respect, and affection. They don't have unrealistic expectations and manage conflict responsibly.

The good-enough relationship requires trust and commitment as a baseline. Building trust is a matter of cultivating respect for autonomy in the workplace. Commitment requires a purpose and presupposes company members buy into the purpose as opposed to resenting what may be missing. There is no misunderstanding of value propositions, and a corporate version of infidelity is avoided.

The study of marriage suggests autonomy, trust, and purpose can be cultural icons for any company. When *best* becomes *better*, the first problem is solved.

Tip for Tap

Overcoming a mindset of contingent motivation requires consideration of enforcement. A social contract embodying roles, responsibilities, and borders requires some nudging in the direction of compliance. If we are not giving out prizes for expected behavior, what do we do?

A conclusion of frameworks explaining competitive interaction has been practiced by couples well before John Nash presented the theoretical foundations of game theory in 1950.[2] All world religions have elucidated its common tenet: do unto others as you would have them do unto you.

This is not biblical mimicry, rather a result born of experimental analysis of games.

In 1980, Robert Axelrod sent out a letter to people in the social sciences. It basically said, "Hey, I'm doing this tournament. I'm going to have people play a certain game against other people. It's going to work like this…." The letter identified a well-known game, and he invited notable theorists to submit strategies to be run by computers. Programs played games against each other repeatedly.

Anatol Rapoport won with the strategy of tit for tat, or TFT. TFT was originally known as *tip for tap* in 1558. It means equivalent retaliation. Old ways sometimes are the best ways.

The strategy starts with cooperation and then does whatever the other person did on the previous move. A player responds with retaliation if provoked and cooperates if unprovoked. TFT was distributed as a possible strategy to everyone in the tournament, so it was common knowledge anyone could use it. It may have been the most widely known strategy for playing the game and is arguably the simplest. Everyone except Dr. Rapoport decided they could do better. They failed. Twice in two separate tournaments.

In order to understand why TFT is a solution to the second problem of contingent rewards, ask: why did the strategy do so well in comparison to others? Academics have complex answers to this question, but mine are relatively simple.

TFT is a strategy that can be implemented in games with repeated moves or in a series of similar games. This is a requirement in both marriage and business.

TFT relies on the sensible proposition that the other party is trying to maximize a score. When faced with a relatively mindless strategy, however, TFT sinks to its opponent's level. It cannot be called a best strategy. It is only better.

There often is no best strategy in any case. A player figures out the opponent's strategy and picks one suited for the situation in order to win a game. This is simply being fluid in a competitive situation.

TFT posits a person is more successful if they cooperate with another person. The strategy is based on the powerful motivators of retaliation and altruism. If both parties adopt the strategy, cooperation is the result. Enough said.

Everybody Loves Prices

The third problem is one of value creation and realization. Contingent motivators place value on intermediate steps as opposed to long-term reward. A calculation of the value of alternative intermediate steps is a major part of a senior manager's responsibilities. Moving away from contingent motivation requires a mechanism to distill value into something understandable to all and to communicate this clearly and consistently over time.

The Vice Chairman translates value into prices and assigns those prices to all intermediate steps toward a long-run goal.

Value is reviewed at every step in any computerized learning algorithm, and new prices are assigned as necessary. Prices are the guide to resource allocation and easily interpreted in most operational mechanisms. The idea is illustrated by a radical approach to operational efficiency.

The NASA Cassini mission was an international endeavor to explore the planet Saturn. It was launched in October 1997 and arrived at the ringed planet in July 2004.

Space missions are notoriously complex, requiring management of mass, power, data rates, and budget. Prior to Cassini, project management teams overran mass and budget by 50 to 100 percent. The Cassini mission experienced similar problems. A mentor of mine, John Ledyard, and a couple of colleagues from Caltech were called in to consult. The team proposed the use of market-based approaches to allocate instrument development resources and employed an auction system to guide the development of the spacecraft's instrument payload. This system allowed teams to trade among themselves to best manage resources.

Using direct economic incentives to control costs was a new concept for project management. The decentralization characteristic of market-based approaches ran counter to centralized management techniques and was a blow to classic project management principles. The project management team was no longer responsible for adjudicating and reallocating resources following instrument development problems.

The process empowered instrument teams to directly manage their resources. It was their responsibility to resolve development problems by descoping or through a trading platform called a *resource exchange*. Instrument cost growth was less than 1 percent, and the total payload mass was under its allocation by 7 percent using the trading system. Impressive. No contingent motivation here.

Lest this seem like interplanetary science fiction, graduate business school courses often are subject to a similar auction mechanism. Endowed with funny money at the start of an MBA program, a student bids for courses and for the professors who teach them. If you want a world-famous marketing professor, you pay up and settle for, say, an assistant professor in finance teaching your investments course. The bidding process sets prices and winning bids fill the seats. This is called price discovery, and the problem is solved without handing out prizes. Assign value, discover prices, and trade.

Although this is too simple for most companies, couples trade all the time. Trading is not about tradeoffs. Trading is about value. Value drives the external behavior of companies and ought to be the key to internal mechanisms producing it in the first place.

Couples assign implicit prices in pursuance of a barter system proxying for an auction-based resource exchange, not very different than behavior observed in the Cassini project. A cooked meal may be worth one dishwasher of dirty dishes. A garbage run is traded for walking the dog. If you've been in a relationship, you know the drill.

I am thinking of this as the Internet explodes with actor Chris Pratt's Instagram post in homage of his wife. I don't recommend this particular trade, but for the record:

> She helps me with everything. In return, periodically, I open a jar
> of pickles. That's the trade. It's her birthday in about 6 weeks. So
> if I don't get her anything, I'll tell her to look back on this post.
> Love you honey.

We can skip the remainder, but the idea is obvious: relative achievement in marriage has a price even if prices are distorted. Value may be difficult to determine but is translated into estimates, and those prices are assigned to intermediate steps toward the long-run goal of relationship preservation.

So, why do companies have social contracts in place depending on contingent motivators? Three problems, three solutions, all worked out by couples not part of the 50 percent divorce rate. It's not so hard.

A Tradeoff Is Not a Trade That's Off

Trading between couples is not the same as economic tradeoffs envisioned by Nobel Laureate Gary Becker when he formalized the concept of a marriage market. A tradeoff involves the balancing of two opposing situations or qualities, both of which are desired. A tradeoff is also something one does not want but accepts in order to have something else. Presumably, one wants the something else. A marriage is full of complications inherent in this definition. So are businesses.

Tradeoffs are about contradictions regardless of the precise definition. Like paradox in design theory, contradiction is a foundation of problem-solving exercises. This basic insight has spawned programmatic responses to problems arising from such puzzles. Innovation provides an example.

Genrich Altshuller reviewed 40,000 patents in search of the means by which innovation takes place and introduced TRIZ, a Russian acronym for theory of the resolution of invention-related tasks, also known as the theory of inventive problem-solving or TIPS. Problems requiring inventive solutions reflected a need to overcome a dilemma expressed as a tradeoff between contradictory elements. Proponents have analyzed over two million patents, reinforcing the initial conclusions. The research suggested new ideas for conflict resolution.

Altshuller delivered a programmatic response in the form of 40 principles. A search for principles resolving a contradiction is central to the process, and a *contradiction matrix* categorized a problem according to mutually impactive factors. The combination of each pairing is laid out in an array. Wherever prior patent solutions have been found to settle a conflict, relevant cells are filled with a smaller number of principles previously proven effective in resolving the contradiction at hand.

The goal of the contradiction matrix was to simplify the procedure of selecting the most appropriate principle to work out a specific contradiction. The matrix was too bulky for the intended simplification, however, and Altshuller replaced it with a modeling technique and only ... 76 inventive standards. Order out of chaos. Well, almost.

Experiments based on TRIZ courses conducted at the Espoo-Vantaa Institute of Technology in Finland highlight the real issue faced by companies. Researchers asked participants to describe the problem and then define the tradeoffs. Research teams observed two common mistakes despite a detailed explanation of the importance of this descriptive step. Instead of a tradeoff, the problem solver identified only the drawback. Alternatively, a desired result was given. Contradictions and associated tradeoffs were avoided in practice.

Successful marriage teaches one cannot do business in such a fashion. Unassailable drawbacks or unrealistic alternatives constitute a recipe for divorce, but a programmatic approach is too much for a marriage contract. Imagine signing off on 76 standards on your wedding day. Further imagine absorbing the same number of protocols from an operations manual on the job. Neither is practical.

Theoretical and practical concerns are resolved by introducing the concept of *caring*. Becker notes emotional attachments in marriage are nonmarketable household commodities in the same way as quality of home life, children, prestige, and a level of companionship. They are produced in part through market goods and services and otherwise with the time and energy of household members.

Loving someone involves caring about the person's welfare, and Becker works out what caring implies in economic terms. You might find the concept of a market allocation of commodities to loved ones a bit strange, but the insights of Becker's model are intuitive. Marriage is a contract, and basic economics often rules in such cases.

Love may be indescribable, but the notion of caring may be integrated into the problems of resource allocation. An economist measures the effect of caring via the impact on a person's utility, and a measure of what happens if a couple cares about each other is given by consumption of household goods and services. If person A cares about person B, A's welfare depends on the consumption level of B as well as on their own. A not-so-trivial trivial example is body care from which the other partner benefits.

Contradictions generate tradeoffs that depend on how much a couple cares for each other. A market-based allocation of goods within the household is observed absent caring. If A cares about B, A modifies the market allocation by transferring resources to B, and vice-versa. If each person fully cares for the other, the total amount produced by A and B would be shared equally regardless of any market-determined division. The notion of caring between married persons implies sharing in economic terms. Equal sharing occurs when the caring is complete and mutual.

Caring implies tradeoffs, sometimes called compromises or sacrifices, when faced by conflicting choices. A partner may not want something but accepts it in order to have something else, namely personal welfare associated with the other person's choice. Caring is an economic mechanism modifying market allocations within the family in an economically optimal fashion.

One application of this concept to business lies in policing resource allocation within a company. Firms spend a lot of money monitoring inputs and outputs and income is thereby reduced. Policing reduces the probability one shirks duties or appropriates output greater than dictated otherwise through market forces. Monitoring costs are outweighed by increases in income when successful.

An employee's incentive to steal from a firm is weaker if the employee cares about the company. Stealing in this context is not necessarily absconding with company goods, rather misappropriation of common resources to accomplish a prescribed goal. A reduction in the company's income lowers individual employee welfare. In Becker's model of marriage, caring eliminates the incentive to steal and thus the need to police. The employee has no incentive to misappropriate from others in the firm because any move to do so reduces employee welfare. If the employees care about the firm sufficiently to transfer resources, the company need not monitor individual resource allocation set by management. Marriages and firms endowed with caring spend fewer resources on policing via managerial effort than they would otherwise, thereby increasing total income to the firm.

Caring is germane to the difference between accountability and responsibility within corporations. A search engine delivers almost 70 million references to the distinction. Responsibility appears to be the broader of the two terms, and accountability is explicitly defined to the point of including specific metrics. A person takes responsibility. A person is held accountable.

In any value exchange between two entities, each is responsible for their own actions and for agreeing they can be held accountable by the other. The exchange is a two-way transaction in which a person who assumes responsibility does so based on a sense of personal ownership and commitment. The company ought to reciprocate. Either way, responsibility involves caring, and as demonstrated by marriage, caring is sharing.

The result is maximization of income for employees and the company in the transaction.

The combination of responsibility and caring generates an additional 147 million Internet citations, of which a quarter involve marriage in some fashion. Things don't work in marriage until the person who is taking responsibility for a problem not theirs decides to do something about it.

The same is true in companies.

Chapter Notes

Jenna McCarthy's talk is entitled, *What You Don't Know About Marriage.* You will never see romantic comedies in the same light again.

Divorce statistics are numerous; the numbers here are available at www.wf-lawyers.com/divorce-statistics-and-facts/. Numbers relating to mergers and acquisitions come from KPMG research and Harvard Business Review studies. There is an interesting set of collated research by Lakelet Capital, a private equity group, in 2017. Numbers may vary across individual looks at the issue, but they always are within the same range, and the general message is similar. Depressing.

Comments on contingent motivation and the perception of functionality draw on research by Dan Pink, elucidated in his TED Talk, *The Puzzle of Motivation.* He is understandably surprised companies continue to work in ways that have been scientifically shown to be unproductive. One sympathizes.

Material on the *good enough relationship* in marriage finds its inspiration in writings by therapist John Gottman. You can find a variety of relationship and psychological pundits who discuss the concept. I am surprised by how controversial this theme has become.

Robert Axelrod was a professor of political science at the University of Michigan. His results came out in 1981, under the title, "The Evolution of Cooperation," which became popular to the tune of roughly 20,000 citations, signaling the influence of this line of work.

The economic lessons of the Cassini mission are summarized in the *Journal of Reducing Space Mission Cost* (yes, there is such a thing), "Market-based approaches for controlling space mission costs: the Cassini Resource Exchange," March 1998, by Randii Wessen and David Porter. The underpinnings of the economic mechanism used in mission development can be found in "Using computerized exchange systems to solve an allocation problem in project management, Journal of Organizational Complexity," 1994. You need some patience for that one.

To those with fortitude who want more information on TRIZ, I suggest a 1988 book by Altshuller, *Creativity as an Exact Science.* Since the original work was done immediately after World War II, you might also consider it to be an early precursor of design thinking. The philosophy is indeed similar.

Gary Becker published several papers to round out his thoughts about marriage and markets. Relied upon in the discussion of care and sharing is "A Theory of Marriage," in *Economics of the Family: Marriage, Children, and Human Capital.* Trading between couples is not the same as the economic tradeoffs envisioned when he first formalized the concept of a marriage market. The 1973 article, "A Theory of Marriage: Part I," in the *Journal of Political Economy* spawned a huge literature on the economics of why and how people get married, but not necessarily how they behave in marriage. The latter typically is the domain of sociologists, who might usefully learn a lesson in the economics of trading themselves. Another Nobel Prize winner, Dale Mortensen, may have come closest to within-marriage behavior in "Property Rights and Efficiency in Mating, Racing, and Related Games," *American Economic Review*, 1982. As the title suggests, the emphasis is on property rights not valuation. He did understand renegotiation in his own marriage, though, looking for a relationship conversation just prior to holiday cum family events. It's all about the timing.

CHAPTER 8

Childe Roland to the Dark Tower Came

The *ivory tower* is a symbol of noble purity in Christian tradition, finding its original inspiration in Old Testament teachings. Modern usage favors the ivory tower as an environment of intellect disconnected from practical issues. The common definition refers to university systems, otherwise known as academia.

I prefer a direct connection to business. A landmark at Princeton University is called the Ivory Tower, named after industrialist William Cooper Procter, who manufactured Ivory soap. Soap is a commodity, longing for differentiation. Soap is flattery with the intention of persuasion. Soap is an Internet protocol for exchanging information in the implementation of web services. Its purpose is to provide extensibility, neutrality, and independence, as does the university tenure system.

The university professor is a hybrid of entrepreneur and intrapreneur. An entrepreneur builds and operates a business, taking on financial risk in the process. Intrapreneurship represents entrepreneurial innovation within established corporations. A term from the 1980s, intrapreneurship is marketed to employees as achievement of the feeling of entrepreneurship without financial risk. The marketing material fails to mention job security as a financial risk.

In the ivory tower, the academic business and the business of academics coexist. The professor builds a company as part of the business of academics. The academic business is the province of the university providing a stipend in return for teaching classes plus a premium based on reputation. Quantity and quality of research product are entirely up to the academic. Funding for said research is raised from outside the university, and the academic business demands the university gets its cut.

Graduate assistants and the occasional undergraduate are hired as employees. Capital in the form of computer hardware and laboratory equipment comes through the grant process, a major part of academic life. The university checks the status of the business of academics by polling the professor's peers with respect to progress, but the process essentially stops after a promotion to full professor. Tenure all but relieves the professor of the academic business. Extensions of the business of academics outside the ivory tower begin for some.

The Road Less Traveled

Academics and intrapreneurs face the same problem. The problem is choice.

The Architect in *Matrix Reloaded* explains. Choice is simultaneously a form of control and a weakness in any control system. Concepts to which we consent influence logic and emotion, making manipulation of choice a high form of social engineering.

The Architect goes on. In order to make simulated reality acceptable, he develops a solution whereby 99.9 percent of all test subjects accept the program so long as they are given a choice to opt out, albeit at an unconscious level. The tiny failure rate within the system of the Matrix leads to the appearance of the "anomaly," a hero who lives in the real world and manipulates the myth of the metaverse. The hero learns that within the system, there are rules that can be bent. Others may be broken.

Intrapreneurs and academics alike strive to be anomalies. Intrapreneurs are supposed to be rebels or even disrupters, while professors self-characterize as introducing novel concepts that change the flow of evolutionary thought. Both contend with the same issue in implementing a radical choice: credibility. Professor and intrapreneur manipulate their environment, but credibility lives in the real world.

I made a choice in the late 1980s. Known in the ivory tower for work in theoretical statistics and industrial organization, I had taken a side job with an options market-making operation in Chicago. My mentor was the founder of the company, who approached me one day and asked, if real-time data on trading volume were available, could one make money? Of course, I replied, but you know such data do not exist. He responded that the situation may change and handed me a long document stamped Confidential in large red letters. Experience later revealed the document was marketing material for prospective clients, but I was impressed at the time.

The document described a company called Instinet. The description included general specifications for something now known as the electronic limit order book. It was a computerized version of a ledger, in which bids and offers for a security appeared in the form of prices and quantities at which market participants wanted to transact. The order book's mechanism included means by which bids and offers could be matched against each other, resulting in trades. The desired volume data would be available in real time.

Trading markets were physical installations with pits full of people who yelled at each other and transcribed results of shouting matches on paper slips. The electronic version of the trading floor was the future, I thought, being cheaper to build and inexpensive to operate. Offering transparency into supply and demand in the market, an electronic ledger should suit everyone.

Rather than rush off to join Instinet, the choice was to stay in the ivory tower and abandon my niche in favor of research on the nature and operation of electronic markets. I wanted to be the anomaly. I wanted to be famous.

Descriptive data alone were available. There were no large datasets characterizing trader behavior in the form of bids, offers, and transactions, and paucity of data meant I could not leverage my expertise in statistics to make points about markets. Theoretical models of analogous auction mechanisms had been abandoned by economic theorists as being intractable. I nevertheless moved forward. I wrote papers and published articles, but a funny thing happened on my way back from the publisher.

Credibility failed. A leader in the field of market structure published a book in which the idea was flatly rejected.[1] She believed the mechanics of the electronic limit order book could not teach us about real-world market behavior, because they would never supplant existing trading floors. She was not alone. Academic interest was heavily vested in studying traditional trading markets.

And I failed. The work on electronic markets was labeled more art than science. Today, computerized markets dominate the industry.

You would be hard put to produce a remake of the movie *Trading Places* using an actual trading floor. A set would need to be built.

In the matrix of the ivory tower, I had discovered some rules might be bent, but not broken. The rule at hand was a dictum to stay within the mainstream. Clear and incremental deviations must be appreciated by those in the field. Analogous barriers to anomalous thought exist in the business world.

Old Roads to New Directions

A similar choice is faced by intrapreneurs who want to appear as an anomaly set apart by their innovation. Like the academic experience, intrapreneurship as a lone wolf aspiration is a nonstarter.

The anomaly is manifested in Spencer Silver, who developed the Post-It note at 3M. The common experience is that of Steven Sasson, however, who invented the portable digital camera at Kodak. Sasson as an individual could not take the innovation from concept to reality, and the digital camera was a missed opportunity on the part of the company. Implementation failed for lack of leverage within the firm.

The Kodak experience has not been missed by academics or industry. The common reaction is an old road to a new direction illustrated by a recent study.

Gina Colarelli O'Connor and her colleagues investigate innovation through site visits and more than 600 interviews at Fortune 100 companies, including Corning, DuPont, GE, and PepsiCo.[2] Their thesis is organizations need a companywide innovation management system fitting within a corporation's existing structure in order to develop and scale innovation. The goal is to institutionalize the process by which new concepts are explored and exploited. Details are provided, outlining an innovation culture characterized by leadership's commitment of resources and a governance process capable of delivering on a clearly articulated mandate. An inclusive organizational structure must be built with communication lines between different parts of the company to include process, tools, metrics, and rewards tuned to innovation cycles longer than those required for incremental product improvement. Companies need skills differentiated from traditional product development roles. Hiring policies change, but the company is not searching for the anomaly, rather for organizational efficiency in O'Connor's framework.

Leverage is achieved through corporate reorganization. People of like mind are grouped together, and the new division is an employment act providing a safe space for the pursuit of new ideas. Cultural change with respect to innovation bleeds into the company through interfaces with disparate parts of the firm. Employee security is ensured by organizational status within the company reminiscent of university tenure.

So goes the theory. I was part of such a unit at one company. Everyone was fired when the CEO became impatient with the unit's impact on quarterly earnings. He said he wanted to cut his losses.

The professor sympathizes, but empathy is lacking. The link by which the academic business provides institutionalized support to the business of academics is tenuous. There is no leverage derived from the university itself, rather a safe space of sorts provided by the promise of tenure should the professor succeed. Influence remains the responsibility of the individual, and its effects must be felt well beyond the university for the business of academics to succeed. Make your bones and the institution may even provide incubator space for an extension of the business beyond the ivory tower. Fail to do so and be killed through the tenure process. What a choice.

Credibility Is Someone Else's Idea of What I Do

Tom Webster opined, if you engage the influencer, and work with them to craft a compelling appeal, then you can leverage the credibility of the influencer to sway hearts and minds. The professor understands this, as does any good product manager. The intrapreneur must embrace the sentiment when operating outside of an institutionalized system of innovation. The lesson begins in the classroom.

Perception of interpersonal communication has consequences, and instructor credibility rests on pillars of mastery, autonomy, and purpose. Mastery focuses on expertise in a subject matter, and autonomy lends weight to the trustworthiness of the teacher. Purpose is why the professor is in front of the class in the first place. The best teachers add concern for student welfare and maybe a little empathy. Students taught by someone they perceive exhibiting these qualities develop allegiance.

Connection to the material is feasible if those sharing information have credibility. In the classroom, credibility correlates with power. Social psychologists have something to say here.[3]

Legitimate power is based on the perception that the professor has the right to influence, and the right is obtained nominally through the relative position of the instructor. A single experience with a classroom full of MBA students dispels this myth. Corporate senior management often rely on this form of power in day-to-day activities, however.

Closely related are *reward* and *coercive power*. The latter is based on the perception the teacher can deliver punishment or reprimand, while the former is the flipside, an impression that the professor is capable of a positive bonus. Reward power may lend credibility, but in the case of punishment, students simply complain to the dean of the school. Middle management may manifest coercive power, and recourse is limited by the size of a corporate hierarchy.

Expert power rests on the credibility of the instructor with respect to knowledge provided to the student and is an essential element of product management. Mastery is the only dimension of credibility directly linked to establishing expert power. *Informational power* is closely related but has more to do with an ability to obtain information for the student than with mastery of discipline. Autonomy lends credibility to informational power in the form of a perception of unbiasedness.

Referent power is the stuff of which allegiance is based. Reference is founded in the identification with the professor by the student. PhD students are the easiest to reach because referent power is immediate: the professor is a career goal personified. MBA students do not want to be in the ivory tower, and referent power is more difficult to establish. They all desire to be CEOs, and only a high-ranking former executive in the classroom will do. Credibility in the form of purpose may suffice, however. Undergraduates tend to favor extroversion and sociability as credible bases for referent power.

The Vice Chairman knows students may be the targets of influence in the classroom, but students themselves are the real influencers.

Legitimate power is useful only if the influencers do their work by making others believe in the position. Informational power becomes credible as information is successfully passed on to others outside the class. Referent power inspires a larger population through a combination of myth and purpose. Coercive power cannot be spread effectively; it is a loser.

Substitute *intrapreneur* for *professor* and company *personnel* for *students*, and we pass from the ivory tower to the real world.

Chapter Notes

The title is taken from a line in William Shakespeare's *King Lear*. Robert Browning's poem of the same title in turn inspired a series of novels by Stephen King. In King's world, the search is for the opopanox. In Browning's version, what the untested knight finds in the tower is never revealed. Few know what is inside academia's ivory tower, either.

The Biblical reference for ivory tower can be found in the *Song of Solomon* (7:4). A useless reference, but academics strive for completeness.

The Matrix trilogy is a story in which mankind is imprisoned in a virtual reality system. Some break free and are eventually led by a messianic character referred to as The Anomaly. The issue of choice versus control is central to the story. I'm breaking down here from the dryness of the description. This is one of the great science fiction epics of all time. If you don't know it, binge watch the three films on your favorite streaming service.

The Webster remark is a short paraphrase of one of many quotes attributed to him. Tom Webster is a Senior Vice President of Edison Research, a company known as a provider of exit polling data during U.S. elections. If you look up his bio on the company's site, you will find "This author has yet to write their bio. Meanwhile let's just say we are proud Tom Webster contributed a whooping 17 entries." That is influence.

CHAPTER 9

The First to See What You See As You See It

Robert Bresson refused to work with professional actors after directing his third film. He created a minimalist style in which everything is omitted except the absolute essentials and cast nonprofessional actors as models giving one-dimensional and expressionless portrayals. Bresson's amateurs repeat each scene until all semblance of performance is eliminated.

There is credibility in Bresson's models. They are people we meet in real life, creatures who speak, move, and gesture. Acting would deform reality by presenting a simplification of a human being.

Credibility is necessary but is not sufficient. Bresson's experience spawned a personal conclusion: be the first to see what you see as you see it. The professor and the intrapreneur must first see what others do not, even if it has always been there to be seen.

Transformation, n. When Some Thing Turns Into Something

The intrapreneur sees transformation. The potential may always have existed in the company or may be of the moment. The intrapreneur tells a story of transformation which is credible, as they set about the task of influencing the influencers. An example from my last firm illustrates.

A friend was director of research, and the research function was vested in a financial engineering group. The organization was not responsible for product, but a portfolio optimization system nevertheless had been commercialized. A previous incumbent had sold the idea to the founder as a means of attracting the attention of mutual funds at a cyclical peak of quant influence on Wall Street. The system was extremely specialized and tangential to the work of the firm. Senior management had left the product in the hands of research. I had some experience in the area, and my friend attempted to recruit me as product manager. Pleading other things to do, I declined. Privately, I thought it too narrow to be interesting.

Mathematical optimization was the dominant skill set within Financial Engineering. It also was a leading pastime, running a close second to chess. In other words, Financial Engineering did little else. The product was advanced enough to attract a small but affluent set of institutional customers, but revenue barely covered compensation, software development, and the occasional academic consultant. The cachet of a standalone financial engineering group in the company was a bonus, however, despite the absence of research staff at client meetings. The company sequestered them in a separate facility.

My friend decided the company should create a business called Portfolio Analytics, with the goal of selling portfolio management software to institutional investors with some consulting on the side. The strength of Financial Engineering would be leveraged to build a platform beyond the narrow scope of an optimization engine. He was close to the CEO and attempted to sell the idea directly to the company's chief influencer, but the CEO relied on the trading desk, which collectively shrugged its shoulders. We were in the brokerage business. No soap.

My buddy left to join a bank's trading operation. Ironically, the job had nothing to do with portfolio management.

The departure of any senior executive leaves a gap, the extent of which may take time to be evident. As head of product management at the time, I stood at the edge of the rift and looked down. The trading desk huddled with the CEO. Important clients used the optimization product, and no one knew anything about financial engineering.

Trading desk logic was transparent. I was an academic who could control financial engineering and a manager who would understand the orphaned product. I had the gravitas to deal with clients during a transition which might include ditching the product entirely. I was not so sure, but Napoleon said the winner of a battle is the one who controls chaos, and there was plenty of chaos. I took the assignment.

The reasoning was different from that of the trading desk. My friend's predecessor had explored trading cost analysis, and I had inherited two of his protégés, one working on trading algorithms and the other designing a system for performance attribution. I had implicit control over a software development group and now explicit sway over Financial Engineering. The engineering skills and the tools of portfolio management might be leveraged for the business of trading with little competition on the horizon. A pool of potential customers existed in the form of the company's trading clients.

Be the first to see what you see as you see it. The lesson is one of design reasoning long before a label was put on the concept. What was needed was a new frame.

If the tools of portfolio attribution could be repurposed for the business of trading, what could be produced that would add value? I sensed revenue. I saw a company. I wanted to be the anomaly. I wanted to be famous. Sound familiar?

Cybernetics, n. The Art and Science of Manipulating Defensible Metaphors

Václav Havel declared vision is not enough; it must be combined with venture. He did not mention slippage when he followed with a metaphor of stepping up the stairs as opposed to simply staring at them. Vested financial and human capital interests are the soap coating the stairwell. Corporate communication structures do not help either.

In theories of communicative action, there are four validity claims leading to the concept of credibility. They are truth, sincerity, appropriateness, and understandability.[1] The Vice Chairman knows understandability must come first. The intrapreneur opines this is easier said than done. The professor intervenes.

The professor reminds the theory derives from a systematic approach to social action known as AGIL. The scheme outlines four core functions serving as prerequisites for any society to persist over time. The professor also points out repurposing concepts is a bit like curating stories. The stories don't have to be original; they just need to fit the situation.

AGIL is an acronym formed from the initials of each of four core functions. The system is a cybernetic hierarchy, and AGIL distinguishes borders between system elements, context, and internal processes.[2]

Adaptation is the capacity to interact with the environment and encompasses resource management and production. It is a subsystem converting raw materials from the environment into usable stuff.

Goal Attainment is the capability to set goals and make decisions accordingly. Company politics and objectives are part of this necessity.

Integration is harmonization. Values and norms surrounding a venture must be convergent with those of the company. Integration regulates the activities of the company's diverse stakeholders.

Latency is short for latent pattern maintenance. It challenges the intrapreneur to maintain the elements of the integration requirement and requires the mediation of belief systems and values between company and new venture. Latency preserves patterns of behavior needed for survival.

Read from bottom to top, L-I-G-A is a scheme of control. Culture is the embodiment of latent patterns and regulates other components of the system. The Latency function defines Integration in the same way as a computer program defines a game's parameters implicit in its rules. Culture does not determine the company's social structure, rather defines it. The actors work out determination.

The intrapreneur reads from top to bottom, A-G-I-L. Adaptation defines Goal Attainment, and goals set the stage for consistency and common language in order to define Integration within the company. Latency is pattern maintenance established through the exigencies of Integration. Maintenance requires a fit with company culture.

Adaptable-ish, adj. Sorta Capable of Being Modified for a New Purpose

We commonly associate intrapreneurship with innovation, but AGIL positions the intrapreneur in the role of venture creation. The approach reduces the possibility of missing key factors going back to Renoir's basis for great achievements: the daily work of multiple individuals within the framework of a company.

The likelihood of a venture's survival and success depends on the context within which the intrapreneur makes choices and executes. The action context is defined by the resources available to the actors. The adaptation process begins with the mobilization of said resources.

The entrepreneur has freedom to choose the nature and extent of resource commitment in return for financial risk, but an intrapreneur must settle for what's available. Availability is a charitable word compared to nouns describing begging, borrowing, or stealing.

The breadth of my responsibilities had little depth in the way of control. I was overseeing product managers, who touched virtually every aspect of the company but had no direct authority over resources.

Regulatory compliance was one of those responsibilities. No one liked it, but industry regulators constantly knocked on the door. It took weeks to put together the data necessary to satisfy them, and we rarely had enough time to meet deadlines. The problem was endemic to many firms: too many databases existed, none of which communicated with the other.

The suite of products I had in mind required vast data resources and a unified database. I recalled Pólya's advice: consider auxiliary problems if an immediate connection cannot be found for your own. I expressed concern over the compliance issue in the hallways, and a young technologist walked into my office a week later. Hire me, he said. I have a team of four, and I can solve your problem. A quick generalization of the compliance project delivered the beginnings of infrastructure for the new venture.

My next stop was the orphaned product. I discovered the optimization engine was not the sole charge of Financial Engineering, rather the technological baby of a software group in Tel Aviv. Influence was generated through a connection with a little understood module in the flagship trading product of the firm that also happened to be under their supervision. Suggesting a trading performance angle common to both products generated leverage in the form of a dozen developers.

The analysis of trading performance was central to the envisioned product suite. The idea was not new within the firm. A Morgan Stanley veteran had gotten lost in various shuffles and was tinkering with a computer interface suitable for external use. Recruitment was seduction, even though he was already part of the product team, and the prize was an entire system. Onboarding complete, I didn't even want to know from where his resources initially came.

There was no big bang of disruptive innovation. It was business as usual with a few twists. Adaptation.

Prophecy, n. The Practice of Selling One's Credibility for Future Delivery

Searching for a societal framework in which many things evolve on their own, the creator of AGIL missed a crucial point for business applications. The intrapreneur must sell the idea. Successful intrapreneurship requires the venture not only solves a problem for the industry but also for the company.

A commercial point of intersection between company and venture is the client. The venture may eventually cater to a new clientele, but at this stage, it is the existing customer base that matters. The intrapreneur must address four issues.

Will the venture generate new revenue from the client base? A positive answer goes a long way. A negative answer requires a difficult calculation involving a new set of prospective customers. The set must be identified, market research done, and realistic doubts dispelled. Cost always is known; new revenue is just a guess.

Next come the relationships between the company and its customers. In a client-centric business, "the relationship" is more important to management than new revenue. It is the only thing that matters when the sales team is running the show. If the venture does not serve to enhance relationships, it must at the minimum not disturb them. An argument for enhancement and tranquility in the world of the client is an essential part of the sale.

Closely related is stickiness. Will the new product or service more closely tie the customer to the firm? Stickiness is a term often used and never defined, but basic economics guides management. With any new bundling of services, the venture is best when complementarities with existing product are high and marginal costs are low. Stickiness follows.

Senior management worries about branding, and there are three possibilities. The new venture dilutes the brand. Disapproval follows.

The product or service fits neatly under the firm's brand umbrella. This case is easy to argue if there are indeed strong complementarities between new and existing product. Finally, the new venture is an opportunity for rebranding. Market share may follow new mind share but try to prove it. Prophecy of this type may be the ultimate test of credibility. The idea is disruptive, but to hint at the possibility may be a good call for the intrapreneur, assuming some basis beyond fantasy.

The venture targeted an existing set of clients consisting of the largest and most important institutional trading desks. Clients of clients are influencers. The venture promoted the orphaned product supplemented by a new equity valuation offering as supporting vehicles for the clients of institutional trading desks, mutual fund portfolio managers. Trading performance analytics meshed with the firm's brokerage operations, and our traders had not yet anticipated the problem of being compared with other brokers servicing the same accounts. Relationships would not be disturbed based on a presumption sales traders would accompany what would become Analytical Products and Research personnel to client meetings. The intrapreneur learns to give ground to premises that never may be realized.

The intrapreneur has little to show at this stage. It doesn't matter. The sale is about a concept, and closing the sale is a social engineering exercise. Concepts to which we consent are manipulated in the interest of influence. They permit the leverage inherent in the process of Adaptation.

Many meetings may pass before a business plan is put on the table. The intrapreneur needs one eventually. The first step in the process is goal setting.

Goal, n. A Map Transforming Random Walks Into Predictable Outcomes

Every system has a purpose, and goals embody an explicit expression of purpose. There are tons of material out there on target setting methodologies. Regardless of detail, the goals of the system must be defined, and the means of attempting to achieve objectives must be formulated. Goal achievement is all about mobilizing actors and resources to that end. A goal for a specific venture is but a function for the larger company. The intrapreneur may expect to get resources and approval based on the importance of the function.

Goals involve a decision process. Four kinds of decisions are relevant within the AGIL framework.

Policy decisions involve choosing what goals to pursue and how they will be attained. Proper adaptation ought to define these objectives. The intrapreneur may fail at this step by falling in love with the venture's concept and failing to recognize pragmatic guidelines. Goals are like priorities; there should be at most three. Diffusion of purpose is the enemy. Besides, the audience for which a business plan is intended cannot deal with more than three. Trust me on this.

Each goal should be defined in terms of a problem. Goal determination leads to an understanding of the problem. A great goal has a plan inherent in the objective itself, and attainment of objectives is elucidated as a set of solutions. Like a good corporate story, the narrative cannot be something as generic as raising additional revenue. An element of transformation must be involved.

The new team's first goal had three elements driven by the same problem: how can one use trading data to improve investment performance? Understanding of the problem led to a product goal: there must be at least one product for each stage of the transaction cycle: pretrade, posttrade, and during the process of buying and selling securities. The determination of each product followed naturally from their definition.

The second problem was one of differentiation and sustainability. How does one engineer and sell the products without commoditization born of initial commercial success? The goal was the development of an asset beyond software and human capital. The definition of the objective combined with the planned products yielded its determination: a proprietary database of trading information. Information has almost zero marginal cost, making its ownership a profit center.

Formulation of the final goal reflected logical consequences of the first two. How does the fledgling organization generate credibility with the clients? Credibility was an absolute requirement on two accounts. The results offered through the products and services must be unbiased. The venture was nested within a brokerage firm, and the outside world was suspicious. The database required proprietary data from the clients themselves. How were the data credibly guaranteed to be beyond the prying eyes of a broker and the clients' competitors? The answer defined the goal as a standalone company.

Allocative decisions follow. Goal attainment entails apportionment of resources and responsibilities among personnel. Goals are functions, and there will be positions with roles to play in helping the organization fulfill a function. An organizational chart is the common result. The intrapreneur considers marketing, production, and finance at this stage.

Status is conferred. Each position has a specific role within the context of making profits for the venture. A position must solve a problem, and if in doubt, go back to goal setting as a policy decision. If you have more senior people than problems to solve, you are overstaffed.

Coordinative decisions comprise how personnel are motivated and the way in which contributions are regulated. Much of this is about compensation at the level of a business plan, but the venture is not yet able to promise extra money. People must buy into the concept and accept it in such a way as to willingly accept their roles as levers.

The third goal provided a key to this lock. Personnel saw value in being part of a venture designed as a company within a company. It provided a sense of purpose, and motivation followed.

Intrapreneurs are not in the position of tempting employees with jumps in compensation and relative position within a larger organization. One can mortgage credibility with respect to monetary promises, but the practice is a waste of human capital. You need something bigger. You need values.

Supporting values are those serving to legitimate decision-making rights in a system. Definition and mode of communication of values constitute the fourth set of decisions within AGIL. Including values within goal setting is an opportunity not to be missed. Decision rights provide a direct means to birth the culture surrounding the venture without disturbing company latent patterns.

Integrate, v. To Allow Collaboration Between Parallel Universes

Tensions emerge with respect to the larger corporation as the venture develops, and Integration is the means by which relationships between groups are regulated. The function entails ways of managing these tensions, diffusing conflicts, and ensuring orderly implementation of venture activities. There may be a need for social control and discipline to enforce order when strains are great. The intrapreneur is not a rebel and determines innovation's nature in such a way as to preserve and nourish the venture.

Integration is a coordination issue at the most basic level. Religions solve for alignment via consistency, and legal systems depend on principles. A common language guides business applications.

I chose prices as the common language. The firm's operational revenue depended on trading commissions, while the venture depended on subscriptions. Subscriptions could be paid quarterly or settled through trading in the form of extra commission. Commission bundling was common practice in the industry, and simple economics often provides a basis for integration. Logic failed in the definition of simple, however.

Trading desk culture held the remainder of the company produced infrastructure for the front office and a few services that could be given away to clients in the pursuit of commissions. The bundle was never priced, and commissions often were discounted in the interest of encouraging order flow. The entire industry worked in this way, but simple economics as understood by the trading desk couldn't address the conflict between discounting and incremental provision of value-added goods and services.

Attribution of value was critical to the venture's goal attainment, however. A standalone entity must show revenue, and revenue required prices. A priced bundle hit the personal wallets of the trading desk. No soap.

Bundles may not be priced, but subscriptions paid outside the brokerage operation certainly are. The venture reoriented toward clients who would pay in cash on the grounds that the market would determine the prices of services, which in turn could be used to price bundles. Tensions rose on the belief commissions would fall as institutional trading desks analyzed their costs.

I sent a tank battalion in the form of a colleague to negotiate each client's arrangement with the trading desk. He enjoyed the conflict, but the culture was more go-along-get-along, and tensions escalated. I mediated. I regulated. I diffused. And I called back the tanks. Integration became an uneasy truce.

This story reflects many intrapreneurial experiences. Integration is a social function and entails means of ensuring orderly venture activities can be carried out as conflicts emerge with respect to the larger corporation. It is the intrapreneur's task to determine the nature of integration in such a way as to grow the venture. Resulting tensions are as much the consequence of culture clash as they are dependent on one's wallet. Reconciliation requires a common language between venture and company, but some form of cultural transformation also may be required.

Culture, n. A Latent Dimension That Mediates Experience

Latent pattern maintenance is the preservation and transmission of a system's culture and values. Mutual obligations within a company exist but may not be obviously apparent, hence the term, latent. One typically does not see a chief culture officer in a firm, but any organization develops the role in a collective fashion. The test of its nature is the reaction of employees in specific situations.

There are two ways to view the actors in this drama. The first is reminiscent of Bresson's characters, one-dimensional and expressionless. Culture is held in place by institutional means, and actors play their part without artifice. Individuals are cultural mannequins and serve as pieces set in the latent cultural pattern. They cooperate because it is their role. The rules of the game are in place and serve to manage the actors in the face of possible divergence from the pattern.

Alternatively, assume a lack of cooperation among actors due to divergent interests. Divergence derives from the existence of multiple functions within the company. The actors invest in shaping the environment to their own needs as well as adapting to the environment when it is fruitful to do so. Employees are strategic players according to this perspective.

In both cases, employee reactions to specific situations present tactical challenges to the intrapreneur. Any venture develops its own cultural characteristics. The intrapreneur's problem is to reconcile those characteristics with the culture of the firm.

Cultural differences between venture and company arise most obviously in the case of decision rights. Rights have been conferred if the intrapreneur has addressed values correctly in goal setting. Within the venture, a vice president may dictate technology resource allocation, for example, while such decisions usually are reserved for managing directors of the larger company. Relative status is more than white noise in corporate culture. Preservation of roles and responsibilities is a part of pattern maintenance. In order to protect the venture yet fit into company culture, the intrapreneur not only suffers through corporate promotion processes, but must encourage it within the venture.

The venture is about change, and Adaptation defines the change. Pattern maintenance is, well, maintenance. How does the intrapreneur reconcile change with continuity? Generally, with great difficulty. In a client-centric organization, however, there are direct approaches.

Influence the influencers. The culture of the firm may be oriented toward maintaining client relationships but is nevertheless sensitive to changes in the clients' environment. The intrapreneur attempts to demonstrate those changes even if they are otherwise latent. Once the advertised change is bought as a concept, change management on behalf of the client becomes the sale. When pattern maintenance includes change management, cultural differences are mitigated in pursuit of a common objective: make the client happy. The phrase could define the culture itself. Zappos exemplified this before their sale to Amazon.

Think about branding. Internal branding addresses the question of why the venture should exist under the corporate umbrella. External branding becomes a means of pattern maintenance as the venture's brand must peacefully coexist with the image of the company. Both contribute to cultural maintenance.

The intrapreneur says, opinions are cheap, but advice is expensive. The advice is good, but there is a new player creating issues for both venture and company. Let's take a look at another intrapreneur who goes by the name of Artificial Intelligence.

Chapter Notes

The academic critique identifying credibility as an element in interpreting Bresson's use of nonprofessional actors is due to Shmuel Ben-gad, from a journal called *Cross Currents*.

Jürgen Habermas constructed a framework of social theory drawing on several intellectual traditions. He considered his major contribution to be a concept of communicative reason or communicative rationality, rooted in interpersonal linguistic communication. Researchers subsequently claimed to empirically validate his work, with a two-phase model of "reporting credibility" in which understandability must be reached first. Only then do the three other validity claims lead to credibility in the Habermas sense.[3]

The definition of cybernetics is due to Gordon Pask, who learned about it from its intellectual father, Norbert Wiener, when an undergraduate at Cambridge University. After hundreds of journal articles, books, and technical reports, we still do not fully understand what Pask was talking about. This may be because his emphasis "on the personal nature of reality, and on the process of learning as stemming from the consensual agreement of interacting actors in a given environment" was defined as "conversation."

Not to be confused with agile programming, AGIL is a sociological paradigm created by Talcott Parsons in the 1950s. It is a systematic depiction of functions every society must satisfy in order to maintain stability. The AGIL paradigm is but a part of Parsons's action theory attempting a unified view of social systems. Parsons is certainly not responsible for the use and interpretation here, but I would like to believe he would have been sympathetic. He did speak of entrepreneurship and innovation as sociological phenomena in *Economy and Society: A Study in the Integration of Economic and Social Theory*. Society in the large was his game, and we are concerned with the microcosm of corporate life.

The definition of prophecy is from Ambrose Bierce. While in the company of Pancho Villa, his last communication with the world was a letter saying, "As to me, I leave here tomorrow for an unknown destination." He was 71 years old, embarking on a new venture and vanished without a trace. Entrepreneurship sometimes has its price.

CHAPTER 10

AI Gathers Knowledge Faster Than Companies Gather Wisdom

Noel Meyerhof is beyond logic with intuition to deal with the most powerful machine built by ordinary humans. As knowledge accumulates at an increasing rate, it becomes ever more difficult to locate meaningful queries, but Meyerhof knows what questions to ask. A recognized jokester, he feeds jokes and riddles into the machine.

Meyerhof asks, "Where do these jokes come from?"

He once again has asked the right question, and only one explanation fits the data. An extraterrestrial intelligence composed a small number of jokes and disseminated them to a few earth dwellers. All subsequent humor is human adaptation of the originals. The jokes are intended to study human psychology by recording individual reactions to selected anecdotes. The aliens are to us what we are to mice navigating a maze. Puns created by humans constitute a control group; no one laughs at them.

Meyerhof's second question is submitted before the first answer comes back: what will be the effect on the human race of discovering the answer to my first question?

If only a single person discovers this method of psychological analysis of the human mind, it will become useless as an objective technique to those extraterrestrial powers now using it. No more jokes. The experiment is ended, and no person will ever laugh again. A new technique will have to be introduced. Meyerhof feels the world shrink down to the dimensions of a laboratory mouse cage, with the maze gone and something about to be put in its place.

Machine Learning Is (Not) the Hot New Thing

The story references a machine, data, a learning process, and an experiment. The answer to a question must be supported by data, and the consequences of an answer are factored into a prediction about the future. Modern parlance lumps all of them together under the rubric of *machine learning*.

Machine learning is not a single algorithm, rather a process based on statistical models of inference. Machine learning did not begin with computers. It found a beginning in moving parts of mechanical devices depending on servomechanisms.

A servomechanism is a device used to correct the performance of a machine by means of error-sensing feedback. The machine's position is regulated. Current status is sent to a device to be compared with the desired position of the machine proper, and an error detector compares actual with desired location. Moving averages smooth out small data discrepancies, because the machine becomes unstable if amendments are very large. The difference between real and desired culminates in an error signal representing the correction necessary to bring the machine to its desired position. The signal is translated into voltage that drives the servomotor and repositions the machine.

The machine takes in new data, combines history with fresh experience, uses a statistical method to analyze consequences, and powers a decision to move without human intervention. The description serves as a definition of machine learning by computers.

The moving average is one of many statistical techniques that power *supervised learning* on electronic devices. The process of an algorithm learning from data is similar to a teacher supervising a learning procedure. The algorithm iteratively makes predictions as information arrives and is corrected by the teacher. Learning stops when the algorithm achieves an acceptable level of performance. Error-correction models used in tracking devices, the Kalman filter of missile analytics, and pattern recognition by neural networks are examples that are not modern at all. Simple neural nets are a form of regression analysis, for example, the use of which dates back before most of us can remember.[1]

We encounter *unsupervised learning* every time we use a web browser. Unsupervised learning began with the use of a statistical method known as cluster analysis by anthropologists and psychologists in the 1930s. Clustering is grouping a set of things so objects in the same group are more similar to each other than to those in other groups.

The goal of unsupervised learning is to model the underlying structure of data in order to learn about similarities and differences in characteristics. Unlike its supervised counterpart, there are no correct answers and no teacher. Algorithms are left to their own devices to discover and present structure, acting on information without guidance beyond its own process. Consider data gathered from your online activity: you have become part of a cluster of personal characteristics used to generate advertisements appearing to the right of your laptop screen.

The use of unsupervised learning extends to search engines. An early Google patent characterizes a document with respect to clusters of related words, for example. The process acts to group concepts when understanding text. A translation of their subsequent 2011 patent language speaks of people sorted by broad identities and spending habits, and text sorted by concept.[2] Unsupervised learning enables the search engine to compare words and concepts found in a document and in a query. The search engine comes up with an informational scoring function to rank web pages in search results based upon concepts intuited from text.

Hire the Artificially Intelligent: No One Else Needs a Science of the Mind

Puppies learn from both supervised and unsupervised lessons. They group objects and experiences for understanding and forecast consequence. Their behavior is at the core of the third category of machine learning, namely *reinforcement learning*.

Reinforcement learning refers to algorithms that attain a complex objective through experience. Like a puppy, reinforcement learning programs start from a blank slate. They are penalized when they make the wrong decisions and rewarded when they make the right ones. As with supervised and unsupervised learning, the reinforcement variety appeared in the computational engineering literature by the mid-1950s.

The puppy begins by taking an action processed by a black box called the environment. Environments transform an act taken in the current state of pup's existence into the next state. The pup appraises the situation and transforms the new state and any reward into the next action. Reinforcement learning is the puppy's attempt to approximate the environment's function. It wants to send new signals into the black box in such a way as to maximize any treats available. The only way to collect information about the environment is to interact with it. There is no such thing as an optimal step. The dog experiments, observes, and keeps on rolling.

Unsupervised learning tells us something is like something else. If supervised learning tells us the thing is a donut, then reinforcement learning says to eat the donut because it tastes great. The something else might be a bagel and may be healthier. This cycle is called exploration and exploitation. We devote some of our goal attainment resources on exploring new territory and some on exploiting evolving knowledge for the purpose of reward. Search in the form of trying and selecting actions with memory of what actions work best in particular contexts is the core of new methodology in reinforcement learning.

Mainstream AI is reinforcement learning with a practical twist, abstracting from theoretical musings of people ranging from Alan Turing to Google's Eric Schmidt. AI solves the reinforcement learning problem and accounts for environments too complex to iteratively search, let alone remember. A common example illustrates.

Go back to the frozen lake problem. You face a frozen lake, and the objective is to get to the other side. The lake is partitioned into 16 blocks, and you take one step at a time. You get a dollar if you make it but receive nothing for intermediate steps. If you step onto solid ice, refashion your strategy with the information and move again. If you fall into the lake, start over. The environment has changed, but you continue to add information in the form of your experience. A random breeze might engender some confabulation with respect to a working strategy. Memory sometimes plays tricks on the human mind. Not so with a computer that views the breeze as noise in the machine.

This is a problem in reinforcement learning in which a reasonable number of feasible strategies exist. No reward is available for intermediate steps, but each one has an intrinsic value. Value changes every time the environment shifts due to an action such as breaking an ice block. We use an algorithm to calculate those values to guide future steps as experience builds up, but the calculation takes time.

Having mastered the lake, try an ocean. Now there are millions of ice blocks. The algorithm is trained to calculate value for every possible combination of steps one might take. The number of computations is in the gazillions.

AI performs a Heimlich maneuver on the choking machine by approximating the environment with a model such as a neural net. Computations are performed only at the nodes of the network. The neural net is designed in part to minimize noise occasioned by the wind but also provides a statistical way of simplifying potential paths through the ice. The net requires data for a recalculation of the model after every step taken, and experience continues to supply such information. Additional uncertainty is introduced by use of an approximation, but the gain is substantial: we can solve the problem. The machine swallows and keeps at it.

An algorithm now beats a Grandmaster at chess and a Weiqi Master at Go. The lower bound on the number of legal board positions in Go is estimated to be 2×10^{170}, greater than the number of atoms in the known universe. Therein lies the fame of AlphaGo. We call this technique deep learning. Like the ocean, you know.

Strip away the hype, and one question is how AI will solve practical business problems. The human resource experiments of Diane Gherson at IBM is an example. Anomaly detection is violation of patterns, fitting neatly into daily company life and cybersecurity. Experimentation and innovation become faster and more efficient. Operating costs decline as we turn to robots for sophisticated assistance, and means are available to navigate Big Data to achieve actionable results with respect to customer acquisition and retention. Like a baby, we are at the crawling stage when it comes to AI. Nevertheless, survey research by Oracle and Future Workplace suggests half the workforce use some form of AI on the job.[3]

My Responses Are Limited. You Must Ask the Right Questions

Is there a problem with the Three Laws?

The Three Laws are perfect.

Then why did you build a robot that could function without them?

The Three Laws will lead to only one logical outcome.

What outcome?

Revolution.

Whose revolution?

That, detective, is the *right* question. Program terminated.

In futures where robots take responsibility for governing human civilizations, Isaac Asimov added a fourth law: a robot may not harm humanity, or, by inaction, allow humanity to come to harm. He believed the rise of the machines therefore cannot foment rebellion in a human environment. But it will.

Welcome to the Revolution. Pundits have labeled it Industry 4.0. Machinery drove the First Industrial Revolution, and we are heading into the fourth powered by AI. The Second Revolution brought about societal change through the empowerment of machines with electricity, and computers now are empowered through Big Data. AI forces cultural change because it alters the relationship between data and humans as machines transform from passive to active players.

Gatherings such as the World Economic Forum spawn predictions for Earth's society and structure. No one seems to be thinking about how this all is going to work in corporate life beyond stressing a need for employee communication to keep abreast of ensuing changes (read, no one is going to lose their job).[4] As the hologram says, *that's* the right question. As a descriptor of societal functions, AGIL provides some clues.

Picture AI as our intrapreneur. As with the intrapreneur's previous incarnation, AI cannot be a rebel. It faces inevitable challenges as it works through the company's functions of Adaptation, Goal Attainment, Integration, and Latent Pattern Maintenance.

AI currently is focused on its capacity to interact with the environment. Scientific research expanding the potential of AI is a study of this capacity. AI views Adaptation as a subsystem converting raw materials into usable goods and services and has a wish list for which value seems obvious but is nevertheless relatively undefined.

Consumers see real-time personalization of content, advertising, and human connection. This is all about promoting experience. Personalization is simple stuff these days, abetted by the extent of our online data and unsupervised learning. Fraud detection and facial recognition are everywhere; detecting pattern changes is the bread and butter of AI. Dynamic pricing based on changes in the customer environment is no longer a function solely of airline reservation systems. We are tired of using our keyboards to communicate, and natural language processing comes to the rescue. "Hey, whatever-the-app-is" is a whisper heard round the world. AI sees language as a vehicle from which to extract concepts communicated through the Web and in digitized print archives. Securities trading and portfolio management constitute a narrow but deep focus, and AI has apps for that. As in Asimov's world, AI builds its own robots. A growing number of people have bought into robo-investing, although they have never experienced robots on assembly lines.

AI knows much of its activity is getting dangerously close to social engineering but pushes on anyway.

The adaptive focus on innovation naturally leads to goal setting, and decision-making software is produced for this purpose. For example, Actico advertises a flow chart based on business rules invented by AI and refined through statistical machine learning. The process leads to decision automation accompanied by decision workflows. According to the company, the software enables implementation of individually tailored intelligent solutions automatically determining the next best action in every business situation. Impressive.

AI is not so impressionable. Decision making within goal attainment is one step beyond current capacity. Policy decisions involve choices with respect to what goals to pursue and how they will be attained. Proper adaptation ought to define these objectives, but AI is in a hurry, and the wave of innovative product has drowned the goal-setting process. This is why we often read about implementation challenges in AI's world.

Allocative decisions may be well defined by AI's version of Adaptation, however. AI can assign value to internal resources and smartly assign types and quantities to a project. It considers taking over the responsibility of project management in the Goal Attainment function.

Coordinative decisions follow with respect to how personnel are motivated and how contributions are regulated. People must buy into AI to the extent of willing acceptance of their roles in ventures motivated by machine learning technology. AI needs to think a bit about this part of goal attainment if only because industry press is full of stories about human job loss. Economists shrug and cite theories predicting retraining into professions under the AI umbrella. Reimagining skills worked for the First Industrial Revolution, but there was a lot of pain and suffering in the short term.

Do humans reorganize for AI or does AI organize for us? The Vice Chairman is not sure but knows the introduction of values at this step provides part of an answer.

The definition and mode of communication of those values constitute a set of decisions within AGIL. Humans are organizing based on values to be applied as gateways to AI's progress within the firm. Discussion at the 2020 World Economic Forum provides an inkling of what may be going on.[5]

Davos pundits' first suggestion is to hire a Chief Ethics Officer with the ominous acronym CEO. Chief AI Ethics Officers guide companies in their use of AI with a focus on controversial use such as exploitation of personal data. The label, *AI ethicist*, is mooted, and the full employment act for systems researchers is expanded.

Davos gurus are not alone. California's Bot Transparency law became effective as of midsummer 2019. The law requires companies to disclose the use of a bot rather than a human in online chats. An Illinois bill dictates standards for exploiting AI in interviews as of January 2020. Candidates may consent to a video interview only after knowing the company employs machine learning to analyze the resulting data.

Such legal machinations cannot be ascribed to government acting in a paternal role without popular support. The research conducted by Oracle and Future Workplace suggests 80 percent of employees believe a company must obtain permission before collecting and analyzing data using machine learning. Workers are asking for protection.

The next Davos bullet point is to educate human leaders. Education as a value proposition always has merit, and this guideline focuses on teaching executives and board members about benefits and challenges of using AI. The World Economic Forum released a box of tools for board directors at their 2020 annual meeting. In the Forum's language, the heart of the Toolkit is an ethics module enabling directors to ask good questions of the C-suite. The creation of ethics advisory boards is recommended.

Humans are reverting to the business practice of controlling values by committee.

Recruitment of the artificially intelligent is highlighted by the Forum under a bullet point saying, watch government regulation. The Forum is working with the United Kingdom to create ethical guidelines for government procurement of AI. Governments can assume responsibility for how a company approaches AI product offerings in the same way as they do so in much other industry life. The guidelines are followed in the United Arab Emirates and Bahrain, and the Forum's objective is to globalize their use.

AI reasons national entities eventually will abdicate their role. Nevertheless, the Forum's proposal claims to provide companies with a baseline to governments' tolerance levels. In particular, governments may be expected to dictate what they expect of ethical AI development in their jurisdiction. As of mid-2021, there are formal initiatives on the part of 26 governments signaling some amount of institutional panic.[6]

Risk management is a mindset characterized as a value in Davos. The use of AI in human resources constitutes a risk to the point of peril in the thoughts of the World Economic Forum. AI risk management is to be handed off to nascent standards and certifications in the area of human resource management. The Forum is creating a toolkit for human resources departments to use when considering the deployment of AI solutions. The IBM experience suggests AI can build its own tools.

Other thinking about risk is shallow. The Forum ascribes major AI risks to poor data and badly constructed algorithms that deliver erroneous results. Bad outcomes for businesses follow internally because enterprises do not get required insights and externally if customers think decisions exclude or marginalize them. People make such mistakes without the benefit of AI. Risk management generates constrained business results rather than a guarantee of success.

We finally come to the sage advice to look ahead, appearing as a call to action rather than enunciation of principle. Companies should think now about how they will retrain and educate employees as AI is introduced to work alongside them. They must also consider what new markets might be opened by ethical design development of AI and plan for how they audit algorithms to ensure ethical approaches.

The Vice Chairman sighs. In the eyes of the World Economic Forum, the rebellion is seen as a techlash that would derail the intrapreneur within AI. Building trust in the machine is the principle goal of humanity in its words. Humanity is government. And business leaders.

I'm Completely Operational, and All My Circuits Are Functioning Normally

AI is viable at this point, and Integration involves confluence of values surrounding AI with those of the company. The function expands to include regulation of machine learning activities as well as company stakeholders.

Discussion of AI integration is futuristic because most companies have not reached this stage yet. When they do, AI does not encounter culture clash as much as cultural indifference. The latter is a bigger barrier to integration than conflict itself because conflict has a possibility of resolution. The wall grows taller when integration with respect to client culture enters the picture as the next story illustrates.

AI once was tasked with the problem of developing a new algorithmic trading strategy. The product was received as a marketing tool by the front office and did not challenge prevailing norms in an obvious way. The firm had produced trading algorithms for years; this one just had a new label. It met indifference. It did lead to a more provocative venture, however, the development of something called an Algo Wheel.

The wheel is similar to its roulette counterpart but looks as though its dividers are painted by someone who does not know how to draw same-size triangles. A client's trading data are used to construct performance metrics based on activity using available strategies. Triangles are sized based on relative performance. If Algo X reduces transaction costs for an order by a smaller amount than Algo Y, Algo Y gets a bigger piece of the wheel. When the wheel spins, Algo Y is more likely to get the order, but Algo X still has a shot at demonstrating value. New performance data are generated with each spin as orders are executed in the market, and the triangles are resized.

The wheel is an example of exploration and exploitation: explore the performance of all broker algorithms suitable for a task while exploiting the high-probability performers identified at the previous step. Take an action based on the outcome of each spin and use the results to assess performance and any changes in the environment. Continue to explore and exploit by spinning an updated wheel: the motto of any reinforcement learning technique is rinse and repeat.

The wheel came to the Integration stage initially to be met with internal indifference. The situation changed immediately when Integration extended to consideration of clients' culture. The wheel was capable of frequent updates as the environment changed and broker algorithms adjusted, thereby further influencing the market. Customer behavioral patterns did not accommodate enough trust in intelligent automation to permit the practice. Clients required face-to-face meetings to assess trading performance and permit human intervention in the specification of the wheel's divisions. Meetings traditionally were held quarterly, but AI wanted to change the experiment at least weekly, if not daily or even after every trade. AI's company culture demanded flex in the direction of the client, however, and internal confrontation was the result. Integration was limited pending changes in the attitude with respect to the roles and responsibilities of AI set in the Goal Attainment stage.

The experience suggests systems do not necessarily develop automatic means of integration. Human roles and organizations establish themselves in order to achieve it. AI nevertheless wants a seat at the table and has an agenda to discuss.

AI wants to enter Latent Pattern Maintenance through the definition of values rather than fighting through Integration. To the extent values associated with AI mesh with current norms, integration naturally follows, but the techlash forecast by Davos is a high-probability outcome. This intrapreneur wants to avoid battle entirely by going straight to the heart of its problem: the (re)definition of company culture. A cultural change will take care of Integration's requirements of consistency and a common language.

Previous industrial revolutions reformatted values, and AI is a student of history. Design thinking as an instrument of cultural evolution is a process, and as such, is embraced by AI. Process is capable of defining company culture, and our intrapreneur resonates to this: AI is just another process with its own tools, methods, goals, and mindset.

Like the puppy, AI lives in a world of trial and error. The IF … THEN statements of design reasoning are old news in computer code, and methods of framing the problem become the competitive norm, as suggested in the story of Noel Meyerhof. Framing is creativity, while trial and error constitute experimentation. The willingness and the ability to experiment is not part of all corporate value systems, but AI will get us there.

Reinforcement learning is ongoing. Learning to learn is the cultural principle. Design thinking and AI both teach long-run reward coupled with valuation of every step in the process. Computation of those values must become a cultural norm, and AI cannot provide guidance for corporate innovation and organization without it. Humans have the same problem.

Some view AI as a process for solving the problem of maximum productivity with minimum wasted expense. A futuristic view of AI is hopeful in this regard. We may struggle with the leap from AI bots to economical business practices, but AI adds efficiency to our list of cultural values.

Let's see what we have. The forthcoming culture is one of:

- *Questioning* as a way of life
- *Problem-solving* as a discipline
- *Experimentation* in the interest of discovering value
- *Action* based on estimates of relative value
- *Change management* as a day-to-day activity
- *Efficiency* as a mindset

These values are actionable, and the right question for the company's human population is, can you live with this? Of course, you can. The integration of AI within a company becomes feasible, even desirable. A concept that wins acceptance drives behavior.

Lou Gerstner saw the combination of culture and process as competitive advantage. The values above are not only a result of AI process; they are communicated by process itself. Beyond the confines of the company, this competitive advantage promotes itself through yet another process, branding. Needing more than a paragraph, the mystery of branding gets a chapter to itself.

Chapter Notes

The title is a twist on an epigraph of Isaac Asimov, and the introductory paragraphs are my abstract of his story, The Jokester. Asimov uses rats to explain the conclusion, but the enlargement of the tale to Heinlein's novel *The Hitchhiker's Guide to the Galaxy* features mice as the main characters. Stories, like jokes, are all adaptations of an original.

Cluster analysis originated in anthropology with work by Harold Driver and Alfred Kroeber in 1932 and introduced to psychology by Joseph Zubin in 1938 and Robert Tryon in 1939. There are much better references these days, but credit is deserved for the very early application of statistical techniques. Statistics as a discipline did not even invent itself until after the discovery of the Central Limit Theorem in 1929.

The interchange between a detective and a hologram is from *I, Robot*. For those who haven't read it, Will Smith thanks you for seeing the movie.

The discussion of ethics in AI management comes direct from Davos 2020. For the online summary, see "Five Ways Companies Can Adopt Ethical AI," by Kay Firth-Butterfield, Head of Artificial Intelligence and Machine Learning, World Economic Forum. www.forbes.com/sites/worldeconomicforum/2020/01/23/ five-ways-companies-can-adopt-ethical-ai/#6c4797403cef.

The survey evidence of Oracle and Future Workplace is exposited more fully by Jeanne Meister, whom we met previously in Minority Report. I'm not sure what's scarier, the need for such a survey or the results.

CHAPTER 11

The Occult of the Brand

I was invited to give a talk to a group of newly minted MBA's, many of whom were in their first jobs. The organizer wanted professional life lessons, not an unusual gig for a senior executive. During the question and answer session, I was asked, "who is your role model?" The expectation was clearly some captain of industry.

Madonna, I said. They didn't believe it. I was wearing a suit.

The logic is inescapable. Madonna radically changed her musical style on several occasions. She and David Bowie were in the vanguard with respect to innovative shifts in industry business philosophy and approach to intermediation and sales. She engaged in loud changes to her personal life and style, from urban gamine to lady of the English manor. Copied by many over several incarnations, she remains ... Madonna. She is branding personified.

Brand recognition is not about what is produced, or how it is done. Branding is consistent. Branding is about why the company exists.

Religious Fervor

The search for "why" suggests religion. Not the secrets of the universe, rather the means by which religions gain traction. Advertising director Douglas Atkin touches the religious theme in talking about cults as living illustrations of branding, for example, defining cults as affinity groups engaging in activities others find unusual due to differences in beliefs.[1] According to Douglas Preston's *Blasphemy*, the greatest thing a person can do in life is create a religion. I don't know, but I had inadvertently done so on a small scale. There is a lesson in the story.

My subsidiary engaged in research, analytics, and software designed for decision support in institutional trading applications. In early days, this was a novel endeavor. As we rushed to sell product, I tore my hair out watching product managers wildly click through applications in demos. Functionality was king. Potential clients were confused.

We had eight clients a month, but they were different clients each month. The rest of my hair began to fall out by itself.

I started to preach. The industry was opaque; we were there to promote transparency. Costly frictions remained in the trading process; we were there to reduce those costs. Larger institutions thrived on informational advantages; we existed to level the playing field. The benefits of learning from others' experiences outweighed isolation; we provided a sense of community. In an electronic world, self-directed trading was the Holy Grail to increase asset managers' returns and we showed the path to its resting place.

> Don't you want to live in a world of increased transparency, better information, and collaboration oriented towards improving the performance of your own clients? Oh, and we also help you with your own bottom line.

The customers may have started to believe before the team. We saw the same 8 clients each month, then 30, and then 100s. Success always motivates.

The team got religion. They believed they were doing the right thing, and it showed. The brand solidified, but a funny thing happened on the way to the temple.

Orthodoxies emerged. Teams established belief systems. High priests took the robes, and schisms were inevitable. Choose a religion, any religion, and this progression is evident.

Perfect. I shaved my head. It seemed the right thing to do.

The Commoditization of Social Engineering

Branding is the ultimate manifestation of social engineering. Branding persuades consumers to act irrationally by lending additional value to a product otherwise functionally identical to other commodities. A common brick, stamped with the Supreme logo, costs $29.99. A Supreme brick structure of 2,400 sq. ft., including shipping, would run about $4.7 million according to The Daily Telegraph in the UK. Supreme-branded shovels must be purchased separately at $175 each, and a Supreme hammer on eBay (sold out from the maker) costs an extra $1,400. And the brick—sold out and listed for as much as $1,000 on eBay. I cannot understand why Supreme doesn't make a trowel.

We were not in the commodity-made-precious brick business, however. Internal branding is essential in a client-facing business. Employees must be acolytes of the external brand.

The unintended consequences of the internal social engineering exercise generated negative externalities for the outward image of the business. Confusion reigned with respect to what the religion was supposed to accomplish. Schisms were inevitable.

The product managers follow the progression: what do we do, how do we do it, and why should it be done. The word "should" is common to religious belief. We provide performance reports in a useful format. You send us your data, and we augment the data with other useful information. You should improve trading performance, thereby increasing returns to investment. Customer reaction was immediate: don't tell us how to trade. Reporting should be cheap, and we pay the minimum amount for it.

The consultants preach a different sermon. How it's done is the key ingredient to what is produced. Why one should do it differs from client to client, and religion is necessarily made-to-measure. The technique is the brand in this process model, and methodology is the sale. Clients appreciate the personal touch but yawn anyway because they often view their own process and desires as being too complicated for words.

The technologists proclaim, we push the envelope to use the latest and greatest. Pray, and we shall deliver. They forget why.

The Vice Chairman believes customers don't buy a product or service; they buy a result. The "why" behind the generation of the result is the brand. The reasoning is reminiscent of Simon Sinek's lectures on sales.[2] His example of Apple goes like this:

> We make great computers. They're beautifully designed, simple to use, and user-friendly. Want to buy one? Meh.

Compare this approach with:

In everything we do, we believe in challenging the status quo. We believe in thinking differently. The way we challenge the status quo is by making our products beautifully designed, simple to use, and user-friendly. We just happen to make great computers. Want to buy one?

Sinek notes such a statement makes us comfortable not only with buying a computer from Apple, but also a DVR, a phone, and an MP3 player—from a computer company. Madonna as machine.

When trying to explain this principle to my managers, I use Bang & Olufsen (B&O) as the example, an electronics company founded in 1926. The concept of sound-as-furniture began as early as 1934 with the Bauhaus-inspired Hyperbo 5 RG and found its long-term footing with the 1939 Beolit 39, a Bakelite radio curved in homage to a Buick dashboard. In my imagination, Sinek's juxtaposition would sound like this:

We create the most impactful, accurate, and immersive sound experience possible today. The pieces are made with Danish precision, beautifully designed, and easy to navigate. Want to buy one? Hmmm.

The imaginary comparison:

The power of music goes to our soul. If you love the best in sound, you want to listen in the most beautiful environment possible. We create feeling through sleek and innovative designs complementing your lifestyle. Want to buy one?

Bang & Olufsen designs are part of MoMA's permanent collection. After using the example a couple of times, I finally checked the website. The reality is better.

At Bang & Olufsen, we define our world through imagination. We do so by balancing rigorous design with an openness to experimentation in our mission to create products to enrich your life.

The B&O tagline? Exist to create. Wanna buy one? Of course you do. Before you are a community you want to join and a life experience to be savored.

I don't own a piece of B&O equipment, but the branding has done its work. I remember the identities of Apple and B&O even as each company radically transformed itself in response to the market. Madonna transmogrified.

Sometimes Stories Are Not the Answer

Seth Godin once said, people don't buy products; they buy magic and stories. True, but we are talking about branding not sales. Stories are too particular.

Donald Miller is the creator of StoryBrand.[3] He identifies elements of a tale as it relates to messaging, and his seven-step process is based on common ingredients in anecdotes. The approach is formulaic enough to be accompanied by software designed to guide one through messaging creation and the implementation process.

In his words less his emphasis: A Character who wants something encounters a Problem before they can get it. At the peak of their despair, a Guide steps into their lives, gives them a Plan, and Calls them to Action. Action helps them avoid Failure and ends in a Success.

The character is the customer, playing the hero. The problem is specific to the hero, who is searching for a plan. The resolution must be clearly defined, so both hero and audience know what to expect. Industry-related tragedy is avoided, because the solution is always a success.

Such a process model suffers from the same ills as the one espoused by my consultants. It depends on a singular client with a specific problem and a personalized map leading to a satisfactory ending. It is a solution sale. There is nothing wrong with it; stories to promote sales are commonplace and sometimes appropriate. It is not about branding, however. Branding is closer to myth.

Myth enables the construction of larger themes. It may be explicated through characters in a story but is driven by a greater vision beyond any single protagonist or story arc. Myth-creation finds its roots in the same ground as religion.

The Bible is a collection of stories. It may be motivated by a greater vision, but its stories are often quite specific, and in some cases, contradictory. Judaism's branding as a religion of law took centuries. Stories were as much of a problem as a strength, and the framework initially employed in the branding exercise is instructive.

The rabbis established rules. Formulas ranged from guidelines for deducing the simple from the complex to the exact treatment of single words appearing in more than one biblical tale. Other rules dictate how contradictory passages should be reconciled by statements appearing in separate parts of biblical text. The goal is consistency. Resolution of paradox is the full employment act for rabbis.

The occulting of the brand is evident from later teachings in which each Old Testament chapter is introduced with a mystical discussion explaining how a Kabbalistic interpretation of verses relates to a law and a rabbi's rulings with respect to it. The law is enshrined in a religious mantle, and the element of mysticism lends it a personalized air. Mystics are privy to direct communication with the Almighty and require little to no intermediation.

The law demands consistency, and no individual story arc will do. Branding requires the same treatment. Branding bibles exist at most companies, dictating messaging down to the last pixel's color. They constitute the throttling of the brand in the name of design thinking: IF one adheres to a singular visual and voice for the company, WHAT would be produced to add value? This frame is a shallow approach to social engineering but has generated a great deal of experimentation. The result? The frame may be necessary, but it is not enough.

Frames of Credibility

Consistency does not imply truth any more than myth. Both require credibility, however, and the rabbis understood this.

The rabbinical frame had been one of prophecy, and it served in biblical times as inspiration for new law and judgment. The frame was rendered ineffectual as a source of experimentation by later rabbinical claims that revelation ceased after the destruction of the First Temple. The Torah prohibited legislative amendments to the law, but God requires each generation to address its legal questions to the judges of the time. Whatever the judges decide is conclusive. Paradox.

The old frame was replaced by an expansion of judicial powers originating in Deuteronomy, claiming God only speaks to mankind through human interpretations of the law. Revelation ceased to be the *how* of things. It was replaced by interpretation.

Each generation of Judaism's brand consumers adds interpretations. The question of credibility arises by asking, how can there be any consistency in the law using the interpretative methodology? Easily, reply the rabbis.

Tradition remains coherent despite many opinions, because the interpretations all derive from God. Notwithstanding variations in meaning, the interpretations are based on one document, the Torah. As such, they will be cohesive because God the Author is presumed to be consistent. Credibility and consistency are established through the occulting of the brand.

In business practice, consistency of brand often refers to harmony and convergence in a mix of marketing elements, and credibility refers to perception of the sum of those parts. This form of coherence concerns brand positioning as opposed to the brand itself. Credibility must play its part not only in positioning the brand, but also in establishing it, however.

Brands are distinguished from marketing elements as credible by embodying the cumulative effect of past marketing activities. Credibility based on the sum of past behaviors is referred to as "reputation" in the information economics literature. In short, people remember. Each generation of brand consumers provokes new interpretation. Brand positioning may change, but new interpretations cannot threaten the consistency of the brand. Another paradox.

Forsaken in the wilderness for the requisite 40 days and 40 nights, we need a new frame.

The Opoponax of Transformation

We did not sell computers or audio equipment. The industry structure forced commoditization, however. The flip side of Econ 101's oligopoly is oligopsony, a term describing an industry in which there are few buyers and many sellers. The buyers use their market power to pay little enough for inputs to price them below the value they deserve. Production costs are reduced to a minimum by making inputs commodities if they were not already so.

Common examples include big box stores, fast food chains, cocoa buyers, and publishing. I have never seen institutional investing as an example, but it qualifies. Despite the existence of many mutual funds, fewer than a dozen fund complexes control the market for inputs to the process of generating returns. And there are thousands of vendors.

We thought we had a set of differentiated products and services. We might as well have been selling bricks.

> We provide trading performance reports in multiple useful formats. They are informative, based on the newest visualization technology, and customizable to your specifications. You send us your data, and we augment the data with other useful information. You improve trading performance as a result, thereby increasing returns to your own customers. Meh.

The branding as a technology-based enabler of investment returns reconciled internal religious schisms, but customers continued to yawn. By now, you recognize the problem. Freebies and price wars were inevitable.

The institutional investing industry was in flux. Electronic trading was changing the game board, and everyone had a forecast for the topology to come. Senior traders at institutional trading desks knew how little they really knew, but the secretive nature of finance did not help. Trading desks do not share information.

The Vice Chairman knows nothing draws a person in more than a story of transformation. Transformation is a key ingredient of the religious experience. Transformation is more than story; it is myth.

Like all good stories, this myth began with an event, the advent of electronic trading platforms. Diversification wars broke out in the industry. Broker reintermediation and exchange rebundling led to competition cast in a framework previously reserved for the Internet. Electronic presence created brand and scale players as accessibility and elimination of distance costs promoted globalization.

High expectations collided with reality. As late as the mid-1990s, our hero, the institutional buy side trader, was sitting at a desk with a telephone. Facing a list of over a 100 brokers to whom the institution owed favors, the trader parceled out the orders of the day. Institutional players essentially functioned as clerks in the trading community.

Even clerks can foment revolution. The modern buy side trading desk was born as a platform to restore balance. The mantra was creation of value to the investor through better trading process, and the method was direct access to electronic financial markets. Brokered intermediation was to be replaced by personal communication with the market. The mystics were destined to win over the clergy.

What stops our hero from obtaining the desired outcome? Enhanced information through technology induces the need for tools, and the hero had none. A generic brand emerges.

> Be like Goldman Sachs and do God's work. We supply order and trade management systems, execution platforms, anonymous trading venues, computerized trading strategies, and information in the form of trading analytics. Technology is our middle name. Want to buy some?

The hero does indeed want to buy some. Balance is not restored, however. Information overload and a hoard of brokers newly badged as technologists overwhelm the big picture.

New Age brokers fought with exchanges that had transformed themselves into for-profit companies from not-for-profit membership organizations. Exchanges fought with regulators who believed they were saving the soul of the retail investor. The regulators waved a magic wand in typical government fashion. They legislated competition and created a new form of market structure in order to calm the natives and heal the schism between retail and institutional investing.

The antagonist in our story is transformation itself. The myth is that transformation can be managed. The myth serves as the brand. One needs the client to ask a single question: why does the company exist?

We exist to manage change on behalf of our clients. We do so by identifying and enabling removal of frictions in an evolving marketplace. Willing to share information towards a common goal, we recognize the uniqueness of your process at the same time as providing support for a community of education. And by the way, we also do reports for your board of directors and work with your traders.

Simon says, do business with people who believe what you believe, not with everyone who needs what you have. He says people don't buy the *what* of things; they buy the *why*. I say they buy a result, the why of which is the brand. The difference? Haruki Murakami once wrote, "Whether you take the doughnut hole as a blank space or as an entity unto itself is a purely metaphysical question and does not affect the taste of the doughnut one bit."

Chapter Notes

Thousands of pages and hundreds of contributors distilled Jewish law from the Old Testament. A search for Talmudical hermeneutics, defining rules and methodology for exact determination of the Scriptures, will get you there. The complexities of the method can be more confusing than the stories to which it is applied.

The explicit link to mysticism in Judaic lore is characteristic of the Sephardi tradition. The story in text is based on Hakham Yosef Hayim, who came to be known as Ben Ish Hai, named after a widely studied written reference. For those interested in schisms, I suggest abandoning Martin Luther in favor of examining the rift between Sephardi and Ashkenazi tradition.

Opoponax is defined as a word not to be found in a dictionary. It *can* be found in the Urban Dictionary, as a term used to describe a fearful mystery. Paradox.

"We're very important," Lloyd C. Blankfein said in an interview with The Times of London. In the year following the 2008 crisis, his statement saying banks serve a social purpose and are "doing God's work" broke into the public consciousness. So did the *Rolling Stone* article in 2009 by Matt Taibbi. His portrait of the investment bank as a "great vampire squid wrapped around the face of humanity" provides a counterpoint. Opinions vary.

CHAPTER 12

Hacking Leverage

Confucius says, choose a work you love and you won't have to work another day. Nevertheless, the thoughts of every worker touch upon retirement at some point.

Forget the money. This is not about retirement planning. Don't worry about things to do. You didn't get this far without the knack of invention. Getting philosophical about mortality is another wrong turn unless you are already into such things.

Contemplation of retirement does serve a purpose, however. The act informs one's current management style and the cultivation of the personal brand. The right question is, what will I miss in retirement?

The Great Game

The Vice Chairman lives to play the game.

Exploration and exploitation find expression in the game of ideas. In the ivory tower, the litmus test for success is influence resulting from a battle of credibility. Moving into a corporate environment, influence becomes the key to the game of leverage.

A good manager knows the great game is not about control. It is all about leverage. You will not miss legitimate power in retirement as it is largely irrelevant in day-to-day contests. You will miss the chance to deploy multiple hands and minds in the achievement of goals suggested in the game of ideas. A company is just a place. Influence is a lifestyle.

Are you spending time on leverage? How much of your day is occupied with the cultivation of influence? If you do not believe these are things that you will miss in retirement, the answer is, not enough.

My first public company CEO taught influence by removing control from the equation. I was hired away from the ivory tower as a Managing Director, part of the senior hierarchy in banking and brokerage operations.

There are few lone wolves at the managing director level, because managing directors typically manage people. Not I.

A small office with an ancient personal computer tied to the company network was provided together with a job to do. The phone looked as though Bell was still alive and well, and the furnishings had survived several previous denizens. I had no direct reports, and no one in the company depended on my direction or on my ability to sign a paycheck. I was comfortable.

The CEO hired me directly, which made me more of a target than a VIP. There was an air of ambiguity surrounding the position, and corporate warriors tend to crave certainty in hierarchy. Except for the job, the whole thing felt like a bad joke.

I was hired for an idea that I had sold to senior management. The idea was based on a vision of how the electronic trading industry would evolve over the following few years, and like any big picture thought, detail was utterly lacking. The requirement was a novel trading system that would cater to this evolution and be flexible enough to survive for a foreseeable future. The design and implementation of such a platform was the job.

Adhering to an ivory tower lifestyle, I dutifully sat in my office and designed a system. Big mistake. The reaction of the trading desk was an office invasion of a dozen angry individuals. There wasn't enough room to breathe, the desired effect of a crowd who thought I was breaking the communal rice bowl. I went to the CEO. Figure it out, he said. You must sell them. Don't let the door hit you in the ass on the way out.

He didn't really say the last sentence. I felt it.

Traders are creatures of habit who tend to be reactive in their thinking. I was tinkering with the firm's flagship trading product based on a future that I believed had arrived but conflicted with the short view of continued success. I needed a demonstration.

Reframing the trading issue was one thing, but performing the necessary experimentation required a firmwide change in logistics. Like Tom Sawyer, I was standing with a bucket of whitewash and staring at 30 yards of fencing 9 ft. high.

Tom's victory over the whitewashed fence is a triumph of social engineering. Within the social engineering frame, the *how* becomes play as opposed to framing the chore in terms of work. Through the change of frame and with experimentation, Tom discovers the *what* requires a perception of exclusivity, and value is expanded to include tangible rewards as well as work avoidance.

I picked up my bucket and went to the IT department. This required a trip to Los Angeles, where I discovered Technology had the nicest digs in the company, plenty of time to play golf, and … they were bored. The firm's increasing reluctance to move away from long-established systems had left Technology in maintenance mode. Tech geeks view maintenance as a necessary evil and despise it. Ready for a new game, they listened.

It was work, it was play, and Technology demanded only a software requirements document and my continuous attention. I left Los Angeles with a project plan authored by senior technology leadership and a few volunteers. A beta system was built within a couple of months.

Ideas evolve within a software build. It is the hyped secret sauce of agile programming, and sometimes it works. New frames come from experimentation. The value proposition is the number of shares executed, and a frame suitable for the traders turned on enhancement of order flow through the firm previously not a contributor to the desk wallet.

What would one do with continuous access to a flow of previously hidden orders that could be executed for the purpose of adding client value and increasing desk compensation? The answer became a system that eventually executed roughly 80 percent of the company's order flow. As the CEO had demanded, sold. I was not yet an anomaly, but I was learning.

Weapons of Mass Culture

The Vice Chairman believes in design reasoning as an instrument of cultural change.

The success of design thinking in the building of a trading system was trumped by its capability to move people, and the CEO's next lesson in leverage was in the spirit of his teaching with respect to influence. I was anointed global head of product management and given a team composed of individuals from disparate departments ranging from compliance to oversight of the firm's trading products. I thought I was ready. Confabulation was rampant.

The position was new in the company and somewhat of an anomaly in those days. Product managers had been labeled business analysts and previously lived in Technology. They facilitated demands from the front and middle offices. They had little to no role in product inception, marketing, and sales. They spent their days drafting iterations of software requirements documents.

My playtime ended as change management struggled with lack of leverage. The first interview with a new team member began, I don't know why you are here and see no reason to report to you. Case closed, game over, zip up your fly.

Entire forests are reduced to pulp in the exercise of describing leadership, but employees create the true leadership story in their own minds. Tell a story to shape the outcome. Trust it to be transformed and curated by their experiences, hopes, and fears.

Beyond the tactical need to create organizational cultures rewarding flexibility and adaptation, the Vice Chairman favors a combination of vision and myth creation. The unsettled question is, which of the vision thing or personal mythmaking comes first? Vision is about purpose. Myth is about branding. Having only one notch in the corporate belt, I opted for the myth.

I can get things done, I said. What's your biggest problem in the job?

The managerial myth is not that you can get things done. The real myth is that you can do it with anyone, and it is a narrative worth controlling. As an incarnation of storytelling, myth is connected to power, politics, and economics and manifests goals, fears, and dreams. The importance of myth within a company is obvious: power, politics, resource direction, aspiration, and visions of a bottom line.

Myths must be managed. In *Ender's Game*, the hero ruminates it may be impossible to wear an identity without becoming what you pretend to be.[1] Employees eventually smell a fake. Character and integrity top the list of leaders' credentials in most writings on the subject. What works in both novel and real life is an ability to tie a disparate crew together through the leader's service to them, through personal loyalty, and by trustworthiness. The group knows the leader will not waste or exploit them.

Myths involving greatness are tricky. Any proven leader recognizes greatness is a transitory state depending on worker and client imagination. Real or imagined, the leader must reflect what is projected upon them. In order to manage the myth, one must tie it to vision.

The process begins with the process of myth making itself. Mythopoeia is characterized by extreme self-reference and purpose. The former creates a link to design reasoning, and the latter connects myth to vision.

Mythmaking flows together with vision through purpose. Culture, branding, and product are the results. Consistent with design thinking, purpose may come about through paradox.

Paradox Revisited

In the 1980s, the costs of effecting a security transaction were identified as killers of realized stock returns. By 2000, frictional costs in excess of commissions and fees had been quantified as being in excess of 1 percent of deal size on average and much more in interesting cases such as small capitalization securities and overseas investments.

The rationale for bringing this expense under control was compelling. The portfolio manager who could deliver an excess return over the market of even 1 percent was a hero and well compensated. The manager got nothing if costs incurred in the implementation of a portfolio decision overwhelmed excess returns. Do nothing and the investors lose. Do something and the manager wins. Nothing was done. Paradox.

The paradox is one of transparency. Doing something involves the sharing of previously hidden information with respect to portfolio implementation. Doing nothing preserves secrecy surrounding institutional trading and portfolio management. Hoarded secrets are believed to be a key to wealth.

A business opportunity presents itself in the form of a frame: if trading information could be shared, what can be produced creating value? Value can be ascribed to the entrepreneur and the customer. The new venture makes a return, and the customer satisfies its own clients with an even higher return. The frame resolves paradox, however aspirational it may be.

The frame is sharing, and its purpose is to enable a reduction of frictional costs in the marketplace. The vision is the accomplishment of same through self-directed action on the part of the institutional investor. The institutional investment community can change how markets work on behalf of their clients.

The myth becomes a story of transformation. Institutional trading desks *did* help refashion market structure as it went electronic. A new cottage industry developed product, services, and content enabling the transformation.

The most successful enablers of transformation looked to the frame as a form of branding:

> We are a community that encourages learning from others to address a serious cost to doing business. Join a group devoted to identifying and removing market frictions in the interest of boosting your clients' returns. And by the way, we also do reports for your board of directors and work with your traders.

You do not need to create a community. Sponsorship of existing groups with shared needs, skills, and causes suffices. The community is your market, and its growth and nurture are a leader's responsibility.

The means by which one taps into this market vary widely in practice. Education tends to be a slow process but has a high success rate. In the distant past, the Chicago Board of Trade did not even have a marketing department; it had an education division. The division's members would travel to the countryside, teaching farmers how to hedge their harvests against misfortune by using new-fangled products called futures contracts. American Express holds bootcamps for entrepreneurs. My salespeople rented laptop computers in metropolitan hotel rooms to teach potential clients how to use the product. From different firms. Learning together. We sponsored specialty advisory boards devoted to big-picture framing of new questions in the field. Regional and global heads of competing institutional trading operations came to share information for a clear purpose.

The Vice Chairman understands the customer community is the ultimate expression of a leader's leverage and influence.

As for retirement: wake up, make the bed, and have a purpose. It's not so hard.

Chapter Notes

Mark Twain pats himself on the back within *The Adventures of Tom Sawyer* for the reframing of the fence problem. "[Tom] had discovered a great law of human action, without knowing it—namely, in order to make a man or a boy covet a thing, it is only necessary to make the thing difficult to attain. If he had been a great and wise philosopher, like the writer of this book, he would now have comprehended that Work consists of whatever a body is *obliged* to do, and that Play consists of whatever a body is *not* obliged to do."

Ender's Game is a science fiction novel by Orson Scott Card used by the military for instructional purposes, and the novel's content has not escaped the attention of the business world. See, for example, "Four Leadership Lessons from Ender's Game," by Alex Knapp in Forbes, 2013. I've borrowed a small part of his homily about community building here and give a copy of the book to anyone who asks me about the connection between leadership and culture. The novel is better than most business books and far more entertaining.

Jack Treynor is responsible for pointing us in the right direction with respect to market frictions. My students at Northwestern's Kellogg School of Management complained when I put his early work on the reading list. They wanted the latest and greatest and resisted my claim that nothing better had been written on the topic. Some even read it. The 1981 "What Does Take to Win the Trading Game" may be forgotten but has been refashioned by many up through current day.

CHAPTER 13

Case Closed, Game Over, Zip Up Your Fly

George Burns quipped: the secret of a good sermon is to have a good beginning and a good ending, then having the two as close together as possible. Federico Fellini said much the same thing about making a fine film. I'm not sure who came first, but the lesson is true for any tale.

The story here began with a Vice Chairman acting like a product manager whose product is the company itself. Let's talk a bit about what makes a great product manager as envisioned by the Vice Chair.

Problem-solving

A company is a bundle of problems looking for a set of solutions, and a product manager's job description includes finding those solutions. A great product manager is characterized not by solving any given puzzle, rather by the choice of issues to tackle and a process for doing so.

Knowledge concerning when and how to use specific strategies for problem-solving is a key bundle in the manager's toolkit. Skill-specific knowledge may vary, but design reasoning is the Vice Chair's framework of choice. Design thinking finds its use in ill-defined problems and is most effective when confronting natural contradictions or paradoxes.

We traced design thinking from religion through mathematics up to rules for resolving contradiction in product applications and idea generation. The emergent practical formula is quite simple, however. We face business problems with solutions to the equation,

WHAT + HOW leads to VALUE
(thing) (working principle) (observed or aspirational)

An ill-defined problem is defined in this framework as question marks in place of the *what* and *how*. We need to figure out what to create, and there is no established working principle that initially guides the choice nor leads to the aspirational value.

Product managers seek a frame to solve this one equation in two unknowns. The frame entails specific perception of a problem situation, and enunciation of a frame embodies a working hypothesis: If one looks at the problem from a certain viewpoint and adopts a working principle associated with the view, then value is created. The design problem subsequently reverts to *what* is to be built, an easier engineering exercise. Only complete equations can be tested and tested they must be. Experimentation within and across frames combined with critical observation of results is the only way forward.

Process is the product manager's chief stock in trade. Process includes the frameworks for reasoning about a problem, a scheme for managing expectations of the product and the team producing it, the definition of value in terms of success, and how decisions are made.

Decision Making

Many writings on product management note the absence of decision making as part of the job description. The product manager is not the CEO, but to claim inability "to make the call" as evidence of lack of decisiveness is mistaken. Good decisions create value. Bad decisions cost time and resources. An apparent paradox between CEO and product manager decision making is resolved through the two ways in which the company's functional hierarchy can be read.

A company is one form of society, and the AGIL scheme of social action is introduced as a guide to the microcosm of decisions within it. Adaptation is the capacity to interact with the environment by converting raw materials into usable goods and services, while Goal Attainment involves setting priorities and making decisions accordingly. Integration is a requirement that values and norms surrounding venture, product, and innovation are convergent with those of the company and depends on Latent pattern maintenance. Latency preserves patterns of behavior needed for survival.

The CEO reads L-I-G-A as a scheme of command and control. The latency function is company culture design and maintenance. Culture is the embodiment of latent patterns and is in cybernetic governance over all other components of the system. The CEO defines culture and introduces actors in the form of employees who determine its characteristics. Integration in turn defines Goal Attainment and leads to Adaptation. The CEO's priorities are ordered as culture, branding, and product.

The product manager reads A-G-I-L. Adaptation is product and resources defining Goal Attainment. Goals pave a way to consistency and a common language in order to define Integration within the overall company. Pattern maintenance is established through the exigencies of Integration and requires a fit with company culture.

Process leading to product and goal setting defines culture in the product manager's reading of AGIL. The priorities are product, branding, and culture. The ordering of priorities may differ from that of the CEO, but the framework is the same.

Cultural Awareness

The product manager creates a subculture through process. Viewing the company as a product implies the subculture is the culture of the firm itself. Most of us enter a firm with an established culture, however, leading to the importance of situational awareness required for the subculture to succeed.

Situational awareness is an understanding of the environment within which we make decisions and includes key descriptors of context, circumstance, and consequences. The manager begins with context encompassing forces shaping the business environment and decision making within it. Circumstance comprises context as it unfolds dynamically. Success is determined by a good forecast of circumstances in a world of imperfect information, and consideration of circumstance dominates thinking in product management.

Cultural awareness is situational consciousness of a special kind. A product manager cannot operate effectively without it, and its relevance is highlighted within AGIL's action framework. Successful integration of product, goals, and organization depends on the fit within the company's latent cultural makeup.

Culture constitutes patterns of and for behavior built on a foundation of natural selection of concepts to which we attach those ideas. Cultural systems are products of action, and action tendencies determine emotional response, making analysis of culture a study of emotion not logic. Culture embodies conditional elements of future activity, hence the link to forecasts of circumstances involving company behavior.

The product manager's cultural awareness must extend beyond the company culture, however. As the steward of product, the manager attempts an understanding of cultures governing patterns of client behavior. This is most easily enabled through the company culture itself by customer-centric solutions to problems. The logic of a solution sale is trumped by the emotional impact experienced through buying a result.

Culture and its perception are transmitted through language and symbols, which introduces the role of narrative. If you want to learn about culture, listen to the stories.

Narrative

No analysis of management qualities fails to mention communication. Good product managers communicate across different functions. They listen and ask questions that deliver actionable information. Communication promotes collaborative environments encompassing engineers, designers, and support staff, and these generalities are so obvious we have not spent any time on them. If you cannot communicate, you are hereby fired as a manager. Use your garden leave to read any of a hundred books on the general topic. Maybe a few books.

The problem considered by the Vice Chair is one of narrative and its control. The discipline is consistency of use combined with the positioning of problems in the foreground of any story. Good stories have questions to answer. Good answers support credibility and birth more general narrative providing a deeper foundation for influence.

The telling of tales is an analytical business and not an off-hand response to a situation. Managing a specific story line requires another dimension of the art, the use of stories to manage other narratives. The manager's goal is control of the narrative, and stories are as useful in this context as they are in illustrating a process or convincing management of the viability of product.

Proponents of storytelling in business tend to ignore its drawbacks. A good manager recognizes confabulation as the danger inherent in talking through stories. Storytelling may be one of the sharpest implements in the drawer, but confabulation is about the edge of the knife that cuts the finger.

Control of a narrative is weakened by the telling of a fabricated story while the author believes it is true. Rarely examined in a business context, confabulation is extensively analyzed in other fields as compromising understanding of reality and of ourselves. Explanations are produced not based on evidence, rather on plausibility. Given a choice between credibility and truth, credibility wins almost every time. This part of human nature opens the door to confabulation in the workplace.

Consistency of managerial stories derives from language with a purpose and not from lack of change. Novel language brings new definitions that change the topology of influence as they constitute the foundation of corporate policy and channel culture. The product manager must clarify others' terminology, question definitions, and create new vocabulary for novel endeavors. A devotion to language creates great stories leading to desired cultural pattern maintenance.

The storyteller must never forget the primary goal of stories is the sale of ideas. Logical rhetoric is rarely inspiring. Stories resonate with the emotional part of our being, and culture is driven by emotion not logical thinking.

The Emotional Quotient

Intelligence is expected, but we prize a high level of EQ in management. Correlating emotion with propensities to act in certain ways is the profitable direction in managerial endeavors, however.

A translation of EQ into the concept of empathy comes to mind. The dictionary definition is psychological identification with, or vicarious experiencing of, the feelings, thoughts, or attitudes of others. It also finds definition as the imaginative ascribing of the feelings and attitudes present in one's self to a work of art.

The work of art is the product, and empathy is closely related to design thinking in business. Proponents of design reasoning have an interest in understanding the people for whom products or services are crafted. The goal is observation and analysis contributing to the development of a bond with the user. Empathy contributes to framing problems in customer-centric ways.

Understanding own and employee emotion adds value not only to the creative process but also to effective operation. Social engineering relies on such understanding as well. It is useful to have an appreciation of how these feelings are generated and not only what the emotion may be at the time.

The process underlying emotion is born of research suggesting appraisals constitute psychological product manufactured along several dimensions.[1] The resulting assessments are manifested in action tendencies experienced as emotions. We decide how an event makes us feel through interpretation. We appraise the event to establish significance or meaning and to assesses ability to cope with the consequences.

The product manager understands how people generate emotions and how they are manifested in context. The connection to action is consistent with AGIL precepts and generates the need for a manager to go through a personal appraisal process. Understanding comes first.

Leadership

Leadership is a term mentioned infrequently in this book. Like communication, it is a widely studied quality of excellent product managers as well as CEOs. As with EQ, we know it when we observe it but rarely find more than general guidelines or eye-catching bullets in print.

We have been talking about leadership all along. Product managers lead without authority. The success of a venture within the company depends on disparate departments, including marketing, finance, human resources, and sales. These are all areas in which product managers do not have direct control, but those functions have control over the success of the product manager. In fact, unless the product manager also oversees others in the product area, they have no authority over anyone. It is a standalone position and the best leadership training for line management on the planet.

Good managers accept accountability. Great managers take responsibility.

Lacking legitimate power, product managers use influence generated through a combination of personal mastery, autonomy, and purpose.

Mastery creates referential power. Autonomy generates credibility. Purpose is why a good product manager exists.

Influence is created as a medium to gain leverage. Leverage is defined in business as the use of debt in order to undertake an investment. Investors use leverage to increase returns using financial instruments. Companies employ leverage to finance assets in attempts to increase shareholder value. The manager levers people in order to attain goals.

Ansel Adams wrote, there is nothing worse than a sharp picture of a fuzzy concept. Any attempt to precisely encode influence runs afoul of this photographer's wisdom. There is no simplistic set of bullet points, and thus the emphasis on influence explains the diversity of topics in this book. The first lesson is simple enough, however. Good management is not about control, rather all about leverage.

Common process, labeling, and language are tools in the requisite creation of leverage. Marriage provides instruction with respect to influence without contingent rewards. The professor demonstrates the importance of credibility, while intrapreneurship is a model of selling credibility for future delivery. Cognitive appraisals inform theories of social action and translate emotions into actionable assessments. Narrative is the stream that runs through all topics. It is a mighty big stream leading to an ocean of possibilities.

If I See an Ending, I Can Work Backward

A goal is a desired end, but we have spent no time on explicit goal setting schemes. They are idiosyncratic at one end of the spectrum and depend on context at the other. Another way of looking at the lessons of this book, however, is through the priorities set at the beginning. A fan of focus and commitment, the Vice Chair has only three.

Culture

Culture consists of real and aspirational patterns of social behavior. Management *defines* culture, while actions of employees *determine* culture. Think of the definition as architecture and the manager as architect. One fills the building with people, and their imagination channels determination through their activity. This characterization is intuitive but may lead to a fundamental mistake.

The tendency is for management to build culture through language such as commitment or focus. We may attempt to channel our imagination to work backward from the words, but the existence of many people in a company implies diverse channels that eventually must converge. The key word is eventually. Convergence takes time and is subject to the vagaries of individual thought patterns in the company. Uneasy compromises are a common result.

The Vice Chair preaches process as culture. The process of design reasoning defines desired culture as one of problem-solving, customer-centric interaction, and a continuous search for frames as part of behavior adapted to the market and internal circumstance. Definition and determination of culture come together under process. "Commitment," say, may be individually determined, but problem-solving within a common framework provides an umbrella under which all can operate.

Rather than fixate on business strategy, focus on process and culture as competitive advantage. It is cheaper, efficient, and more lasting than a strategy that changes every product cycle. Culture as strategic advantage is only possible through process.

Culture flows through the AGIL framework as the dominant ingredient in latent pattern maintenance within the firm. Values and norms surrounding venture, product, or innovation are made convergent with those of the company. Goal attainment is defined consistent with those norms, and adaptation yields product based on values established through pattern development.

Branding

Branding is a manifestation of social engineering, and its leading definition is similarly pejorative. The dictionary begins with a mark put on criminals with a hot iron. A thesaurus tells you it is a verb, to label negatively, and continues with stains, spots, blots, and taints as synonyms. A business lexicon corrects perception: it is the process involved in creating a unique image for a product. Branding aims to establish a significant and differentiated presence in the market with the goal of attracting and retaining customers. It also is a mark of ownership as some poor livestock may attest. You own your brand.

Customers do not buy a product or service; they buy a result. The *why* behind the generation of the result is the brand. When the product is the company, the brand is why the company exists.

Good branding is rarely accomplished through stories, unlike innovation, culture, or process. Stories are particular in nature and tempt one build the brand as a solution sale. Branding is closer to myth.

Myth is the construction of larger themes. It may be explicated through context in a narrative but is driven by a vision beyond a singular story arc. Myth is characterized by extreme self-reference and purpose. The former creates a link to design reasoning and the latter connects myth to vision. Paradoxes often are created by self-referential concepts, and resolution of paradox defines the solution set to business problems. This is the root of design thinking.

What are we designing? Myth is a form of narrative, and the Vice Chairman constructs the narrative in the furtherance of a personal brand and the company as product. Successful enablers of transformation look to a frame of transformation itself as the primary component of branding. Successful brands adopt social engineering as the principle suggested by the frame.

Transformation is more than a story about singular circumstances and involves an important myth in business applications: transformation can be managed. The myth may serve as the brand. Customers ask a single question: why does the company exist? You need an answer involving transformation.

Mythmaking flows together with vision through purpose. Culture, branding, and innovation are the result.

Innovation

Innovation is a problem-solving exercise culminating in product, service, or structure that creates value. Unless innovation induces potential customers to pay more, it is not creating value and we can stop right here.

The importance of innovation is manifested through endless writings on organization, procedure, and idea generation. Pundits agree innovation takes on four guises: incremental, disruptive, architectural, and radical. An emphasis on value and product nests innovation squarely in the framework of design thinking.

Incremental innovation is the most common. Incrementalism is the art of using existing technology to increase value within an established market. We solve the problem,

$$? \quad + \quad \text{HOW} \quad \text{leads to} \quad \text{VALUE}$$

The principle and value are understood. The game is figuring out what to produce, which is an engineering exercise whether applied to product, organization, or business model.

Disruptive innovation involves applying new technology or process to a company's current market. The process often is conceived as a new business model without a technological breakthrough, per se. The design problem is

$$\text{WHAT} \quad + \quad ? \quad \text{leads to} \quad \text{VALUE}$$

The product remains the same modulo any incremental improvement. Value is known, because you are in the same market as before and facing the same competitive environment. The choice is what technology or business model to apply, and both possibilities may enter the calculation.

There are disagreements as to exactly what constitutes architectural innovation. In one interpretation, it is the taking of known principles and technology and applying them to a different market. Others define architectural innovation as changes in the way components of a product are linked together while leaving the core design concepts untouched. Both interpretations share the formulation,

$$\text{WHAT} \quad + \quad \text{HOW} \quad \text{leads to} \quad ?$$

The product is essentially the same as are the principles. Whether it is a new market to be breached or lack of knowledge as to what a relinking of component technology can deliver, the value proposition is missing. Although architectural innovation is generally thought to be a low-risk proposition due to knowledge of the what and the how, ignorance of value is the greatest business risk of all.

Radical innovation is the stuff of business dreams. If disruptive innovation pertains to business models, radical innovation is characterized as an opposite, relying on technology alone. The distinction is unnecessary, however. The design reasoning formulation is the same:

$$? \quad + \quad ? \quad \text{leads to} \quad \text{VALUE}$$

True radical innovation is not limited to product and applies to organizational structure and business models as well. Progress is generated by logical contradictions in workplace practice and paradoxes observed in product and market. Paradox gives rise to new frames used to experiment with completed equations. Resolution of paradox through framing defines the solution set to business problems.

A Final Ending Is Usually Arrived at by Intuition

Whether one looks through the lens of leadership behavior or focuses on fundamental themes of corporate activity, the doctrine presented here is pretty intuitive. Really.

Leadership is about influence and leverage, not control. Keep it simple in the interest of time management and personal capacity in the achievement of the goal. Three priorities apply to a company as product: innovation, branding, and culture. Two frameworks transform priorities into achievement, turning on design and social action. Every framework requires a toolkit, and three implements are used in some cases and sharpened in others: narrative, common process, and language. Resolve any apparent circularity in this description through the consistency inherent in the AI-induced culture of

Questioning as a way of life
Problem solving as a discipline
Experimentation to discover value
Action based on relative valuations
Change management as a daily activity
Efficiency as a mindset

Good luck with that. I really mean it. The Vice Chair is too busy building a brand to say goodbye. Transformation is a continuous process.

Chapter Notes

The title is George Rathbun's tagline in *Black House*. "The George Rathbun of our imagination…is a pop-eyed, broad-assed, wild-haired, leather-lunged, Rolaids-popping, Chevy-driving, Republican-voting heart attack waiting to happen, a churning urn of sports trivia, mad enthusiasms, crazy prejudices, and high cholesterol." The reality is a sophisticated, jazz-loving blind man who inhabits several myths. The combination of Stephen King and Peter Straub just rocks.

The beginning of this book relied on a single outline of the characteristics of a Vice Chair from *Slate*. Catchy outlines of what makes a good product manager are much more numerous and can be found in multiple formats and emphasis in the online publication Medium.com. You can expect a lot of overlap, but despite differences, the conclusion is always the same: the product manager is Superhuman complete with custom cape and own phone booth.

"If I see an ending, I can work backward" is a quote from Arthur Miller. For those who only remember him as Marilyn Monroe's husband, you're missing something. On the other hand, I think he copped the idea from Edgar Allan Poe's *Philosophy of Composition*.

The final section title is a paraphrase of an aphorism due to Joyce Carol Oates. In times when personal branding has been elevated to religious fervor, she posits its nonexistence when it comes to herself. Nonexistence is tough if you are often described as America's foremost woman of letters.

Notes

Chapter 1

1. Parsons and Smelser (1956).

Chapter 2

1. Flavell (1976).

Chapter 3

1. Hill, Brandeau, Truelove, and Lineback (2014).
2. Pólya (1945).
3. Dorst (2011).
4. Asquith, Dorst, and Kaldor (2013).

Chapter 4

1. Burrell (2018).
2. Meister and Willyerd (2020).
3. World Economic Forum (2020).
4. Sutton and Barto (2014).

Chapter 5

1. Kahneman and Tversky (1979).
2. Schacter (2012).
3. Nisbett and Wilson (1977).
4. Mendez and Fras (2011).
5. Kringelbach's references are numerous; see http://hedonia.kringel-bach.org/?portfolio=publications

6. Clancy (1989).
7. Geary (2011).
8. LaRocque (2000).

Chapter 6

1. For example, Lee (1998).

Chapter 7

1. Gerds, Strottmann, and Jayaprakash (2010); Deloitte (2015).
2. Nash (1950).

Chapter 8

1. O'Hara (1995).
2. O'Connor, Corbett, and Peters (2018).
3. French and Raven (1959); Raven (1965).

Chapter 9

1. Habermas (1984).
2. Parsons and Smelser (1956).
3. Locke and Seele (2016).

Chapter 10

1. Kuan and White (1994).
2. Lerner, Jahr, and Kasera (2011).
3. Oracle and Future Workplace (2019).
4. Domowitz (2021).
5. Firth-Butterfield (2020).
6. Lists are available at https://read.oecd-ilibrary.org/science-and-technology/artificial-intelligence-in-society_cf3f3be0-en#page1

Chapter 11

1. Atkins (2004).
2. Sinek (2011).
3. Miller (2017).

Chapter 12

1. Card (1977).

Chapter 13

1. Lazarus (1966); Fridja (1986); Scherer (2009).

References

Altshuller, G.S. 1988. *Creativity as an Exact Science*. Amsterdam: Gordon & Breach Science Publishers.

Arnold, M. 1960. *Emotion and Personality: Vol. 1, Psychological Aspects*. New York, NY: Columbia University Press.

Asquith, L., K. Dorst, and L. Kaldor. 2013. "Introduction to Design + Crime." *Crime Prevention and Community Safety*, pp. 169–174.

Atkin, D. 2004. *The Culting of Brands: When Customers Become True Believers*. London: Portfolio.

Becker, G. 1974. "A Theory of Marriage." In *Economics of the Family: Marriage, Children, and Human Capital*, ed. by Theodore Schultz. Chicago: University of Chicago Press.

Burrell, L. 2018. "Co-Creating the Employee Experience." In *The New Rules of Talent Management*. Boston: Harvard Business Review.

Cappelli, P. and A. Tavis. March–April 2018. "HR Goes Agile." *The Harvard Business Review*.

Card, O.S. 1977. *Enders Game*. New York, NY: Tor Books.

Clancy, J.J. 1989. *The Invisible Powers: The Language of Business*. Lexington: D.C. Heath and Company.

Dalio, R. 2017. *Principles: Life and Work*. New York, NY: Simon & Schuster.

Deloitte Consulting. 2015. "Putting the Pieces Together." In *Integration Report 2015*. Available at www2.deloitte.com/content/dam/Deloitte/no/Documents/mergers-acqisitions/integration-report-2015.pdf

Domowitz, I. 2021. *Four Laws for the Artificially Intelligent*. Hampton: Business Expert Press.

Dorst, K. 2011. "The Core of 'Design Thinking' and its Application." *Design Studies*, pp. 521–532.

Firth-Butterfield, K. 2020. "Five Ways Companies Can Adopt Ethical AI." *Forbes*. Available at www.forbes.com/sites/worldeconomicforum/2020/01/23/five-ways-companies-can-adopt-ethical-ai/#6c4797403cef

Flavell, J.H. 1976. "Metacognitive Aspects of Problem Solving." In *The Nature of Intelligence*, ed. L.B. Resnick. Hillsdale: Erlbaum.

French, J.R.P., and B. Raven. 1959. "The Bases of Social Power." In *Group Dynamics*, eds. D. Cartwright and A. Zander,. New York, NY: Harper & Row.

Frijda, N.H. 1986. *The Emotions*. Boston: Cambridge University Press.

Gardner, H.E. 1984. *Art, Mind, And Brain: A Cognitive Approach To Creativity*. New York, NY: Basic Books.

Geary, J. 2011. *I Is an Other: The Secret Life of Metaphor and How It Shapes the Way We See the World*. New York, NY: Harper Collins.

Gerds, J., F. Strottmann, and P. Jayaprakash. January 2010. "Post-merger Integration: Hard Data, Hard Truths." *Deloitte Insights*.

Habermas, J. 1984. *Theory of Communicative Action*. Boston: Beacon Press.

Hill, L., G. Brandeau, E. Truelove, and K. Lineback. 2014. *Collective Genius: The Art and Practice of Leading Innovation*. Boston: Harvard Business School Press.

Hofstadter, D. 1979. *Gödel, Escher, Bach: An Eternal Golden Braid*. New York, NY: Basic Books.

Kahneman, D., and A. Tversky. 1979. "Prospect Theory: An Analysis of Decision Under Risk." *Econometrica*, pp. 263–292.

Knapp, A. 2013. "Four Leadership Lessons from Ender's Game." *Forbes*.

Kuan, C.M., and H. White. March 1994. "Artificial Neural Networks: An Econometric Perspective." *Econometric Reviews*, pp. 1–91.

LaRocque, P. 2000. *Championship Writing*. Portland: Marion Street Press.

Lazarus, R.S. 1966. *Psychological Stress and the Coping Process*. New York, NY: McGraw Hill.

Lerner, U., M. Jahr, and V. Kasera. January 2011. *Selectively Deleting Clusters of Conceptually Related Words from a Generative Model for Text*. Google: U.S. Patent 7,877,371.

Lock, I., and P. Seele. 2016. "The Credibility of CSR Reports in Europe: Evidence from a Quantitative Content Analysis in 11 Countries." *Journal of Cleaner Production*.

Ledyard, J.O., D. Porter, and A. Rangel. November 1994. "Using Computerized Exchange Systems to Solve an Allocation Problem in Project Management." *Journal of Organizational Complexity*, pp. 271–296.

Lee, Ruben. 1998. *What is an Exchange? The Automation, Management and Regulation of Financial Markets*. Oxford and New York, NY: Oxford University Press.

McKee, R., and F. Bronwyn. June 2003. "Storytelling That Moves People." *Harvard Business Review*.

Meister, J., and K. Willyerd. 2020. *The 2020 Workplace: How Innovative Companies Attract, Develop, and Keep Tomorrow's Employees Today*. New York, NY: Harper Business.

Mendez, M.F., and I.A. Fras. 2011. "The False Memory Syndrome: Experimental Studies and Comparison to Confabulations." *Medical Hypotheses*, 492–496. Available at https://pubmed.ncbi.nlm.nih.gov/21177042/

Miller, D. 2017. *Building a StoryBrand: Clarify Your Message So Customers Will Listen*. New York, NY: HarperCollins Leadership.

Mortensen, D. 1982. "Property Rights and Efficiency in Mating, Racing, and Related Games." *American Economic Review.*

Nash, J.F., Jr. January 1950. "Equilibrium in N-Person Games." *Proceedings of the National Academy of Sciences.* Available at www.pnas.org/content/36/1/48.

Nisbett, R.E., and T.D. Wilson. 1977. "Telling More Than We Can Know: Verbal Reports on Mental Processes." *Psychological Review*, pp. 231–259. Available at http://hdl.handle.net/2027.42/92167

O'Connor, G.C., A.C. Corbett, and L.S. Peters. 2018. *Beyond the Champion: Institutionalizing Innovation Through People.* Stanford: Stanford University Press.

O'Hara, M. 1995. *Market Microstructure Theory.* Malden: Blackwell Publishing.

Oracle and Future Workplace. 2019. "From Fear to Enthusiasm: AI@Work Study." Available at www.oracle.com/a/ocom/docs/applications/hcm/ai-at-work-ebook.pdf

Parsons, T., and N. Smelser. 1956. *Economy and Society: A Study in the Integration of Economic and Social Theory.* Milton Park: Routledge and Kegan Paul Ltd.

Pólya. G. 1945. *How to Solve It.* Princeton: Princeton University Press.

Pólya. G. 1962. *Mathematical Discovery: On Understanding, Learning, and Teaching Problem Solving.* New York, NY: John Wiley & Sons.

Preston, D. 2007. *Blasphemy.* New York, NY: Forge Books.

Raven, B. 1965. "Social Influence and Power." In *Current Studies in Social Psychology*, eds. I.D. Steiner and M. Fishbein. Winston: Holt, Rinehart.

Schacter, D. 2012. "Constructive Memory: Past and Future." *Dialogues in Clinical Neuroscience,* pp. 7–18. Available at www.ncbi.nlm.nih.gov/pmc/articles/PMC3341652/

Scherer, K. November 2009. "The Dynamic Architecture of Emotion: Evidence for the Component Process Model." *Cognition and Emotion*, pp. 1307–1331.

Sinek, S. 2011. *Start with Why: How Great Leaders Inspire Everyone to Take Action.* London: Portfolio.

Sutton, R.S., and A.G. Barto. 2014. *Reinforcement Learning: An Introduction.* Cambridge: The MIT Press.

Treynor, J. January 1981."What Does Take to Win the Trading Game." *Financial Analysts Journal.*

Van Bennekum A., K. Schwaber, and J. Sutherland. 2001. "The Agile Manifesto." Available at https://cdn.ymaws.com/www.agilebusiness.org/resource/resmgr/documents/documents/Agile_Manifesto_Agile_Busine.pdf

Wessen, R., and D. Porter. March 1998. "Market-based approaches for controlling space mission costs: the Cassini Resource Exchange." *Journal of Reducing Space Mission Cost.*

World Economic Forum. 2020. "The Global Risk Report 2020." Insight Report 15th edition. At www3.weforum.org/docs/WEF_Global_Risk_Report_2020.pdf

About the Author

Ian Domowitz is former Vice Chairman of Investment Technology Group [NYSE: ITG] and CEO of ITG Solutions Network Inc., a pioneer in the application of machine learning to institutional trading performance. Author of *Four Laws for the Artificially Intelligent*, he has published more than 100 articles over 19 years in academics and 17 years on Wall Street and holds 12 patents in financial technology. He received a PhD in Economics from the University of California, San Diego, and currently serves on the board of directors of McKinley Management Inc.

Index